The Future Horizon for a Prophetic Tradition

Missional Church, Public Theology, World Christianity

Stephen Bevans, Paul S. Chung, Veli-Matti Kärkkäinen
and Craig L. Nessan, Series Editors

IN THE MIDST OF globalization there is crisis as well as opportunity. A model of God's mission is of special significance for ecclesiology and public theology when explored in diverse perspectives and frameworks in the postcolonial context of World Christianity. In the face of the new, complex global civilization characterized by the Second Axial Age, the theology of mission, missional ecclesiology, and public ethics endeavor to provide a larger framework for missiology. It does so in interaction with our social, multicultural, political, economic, and intercivilizational situation. These fields create ways to refurbish mission as constructive theology in critical and creative engagement with cultural anthropology, world religions, prophetic theology, postcolonial hermeneutics, and contextual theologies of World Christianity. Such endeavors play a critical role in generating theological, missional, social-ethical alternatives to the reality of Empire—a reality characterized by civilizational conflict, and by the complex system of a colonized lifeworld that is embedded within practices of greed, dominion, and ecological devastation. This series—Missional Church, Public Theology, World Christianity—invites scholars to promote alternative church practices for life-enhancing culture and for evangelization as telling the truth in the public sphere, especially in solidarity with those on the margins and in ecological stewardship for the lifeworld.

The Future Horizon for a Prophetic Tradition

A Missiological, Hermeneutical, and Leadership Approach to Education and Black Church Civic Engagement

David L. Everett

PICKWICK Publications • Eugene, Oregon

The FUTURE FOR A PROPHETIC TRADITION
A Missiological, Hermeneutical, and Leadership Approach to Education and Black Church Civic Engagement

Missional Church, Public Theology, World Christianity 7

Copyright © 2017 David L. Everett. All rights reserved. Except for brief quotations in critical publications or reviews, no part of this book may be reproduced in any manner without prior written permission from the publisher. Write: Permissions, Wipf and Stock Publishers, 199 W. 8th Ave., Suite 3, Eugene, OR 97401.

Pickwick Publications
An Imprint of Wipf and Stock Publishers
199 W. 8th Ave., Suite 3
Eugene, OR 97401

www.wipfandstock.com

PAPERBACK ISBN: 978-1-4982-7862-1
HARDCOVER ISBN: 978-1-4982-7864-5
EBOOK ISBN: 978-1-4982-7863-8

Cataloguing-in-Publication data:

Names: Everett, David L.

Title: The future for a prophetic tradition : a missiological, hermeneutical, and leadership approach to education and black church civic engagement | David L. Everett

Description: Eugene, OR: Pickwick Publications, 2017 | Missional Church, Public Theology, World Christianity 7 | Includes bibliographical references.

Identifiers: ISBN 978-1-4982-7862-1 (paperback) | ISBN 978-1-4982-7864-5 (hardcover) | ISBN 978-1-4982-7863-8 (ebook)

Subjects: Church and social problems—United States. | African American churches. | Church and education—United States. | Christian leadership. | Mission of the church. | Prophecy—Social aspects—United States.

Classification: LCC BR563.N4 E8 2017 (print) | LCC BR563.N4 (ebook)

Manufactured in the U.S.A.   MARCH 16, 2017

This is dedicated to my mother Janette who cultivated and nourished everything in me that God planted and continues to blossom.
Even even when I don't see.

I love you and miss you dearly.

Contents

Introduction | ix

Chapter One   Setting the Stage | 1
Chapter Two   Interpretative Dilemma | 18
Chapter Three   Contextual Shaping | 43
Chapter Four   Moving Forward | 68
Chapter Five   Conclusion | 92

Bibliography | 103

Introduction

> "I prayed for freedom for twenty years, but received no answer until I prayed with my legs."
>
> FREDERICK DOUGLASS

So how does a young, Black male from upstate New York who grew up with a militant single mother with no church affiliation get to the pulpit and place of critiquing the most long-standing, historic pillar in the Black community? I ask myself this question as I sit in yet another church reception area, waiting on yet another pastor, to conduct yet another interview, to get yet another perspective on the premise, promise, and plight of the historic Black Church. Having grown up without a "membership" in the Black Church, but without a doubt falling under its mission within the Black community, my experience for many years was simultaneously distant and distinct. On the one hand, the occasional functions such as picnics, christenings, funerals, weddings, and car washes are very memorable. They served as bright spots in a very dark community and childhood riddled with drugs, physical abuse, and financial instability. And yet, on the other hand, those occasional functions did little to nothing to address the darkness of the community as I knew and experienced it.

Interview after interview, I ask the ultimate question, "What is the role of the Black Church?" For the most part, I get similar responses—either being "a prophetic voice," "championing the needs of the community," or "providing a training ground for Black children and support network for the Black community." As a result, I wanted to evaluate the effectiveness of, and opportunities for, the historic Black Church to either maintain its position within the Black community, or reestablish itself as a viable contributor to the Black community's economic, political and social engagement with society at-large.

Ultimately, I believe that understanding the role that the historic Black Church may play requires a fundamental understanding and acceptance of the role that race and inequities still play in American society. While the Unites States is more equal in terms of ethnic and gender demographics, the inequities that exist across those same distinctions are astounding—from income gaps, to incarceration rates, to expected life span. Additionally, subsequent overlap associated with these inequities reflect the kinds of activities that plagued the Black community in the early 1950s and 60s. The rise in racial encounters, or least occurrences that appear to have racial undertones, stand as defining features of American society today and pivotal moments for the Black Church.

Black Church & Civic Engagement

From its introduction in the late 1960s, the term *Black Church* has been a point of debate for many African-American scholars and historians. Some use the term as sociological and theological shorthand to express the pluralism of Black Christian churches in the United States,[1] while others argue that the term is a political, intellectual, and theological construction that masks the enormous diversity and independence among African-American religious institutions and believers.[2] On both sides of the debate, common ground exists in the identification and recognition of multiple religious expressions among the Black Church. On that basis, this contribution contends that *the* Black Church has existed and continues to exist as a fellowship of churches organized by their Christianity, vitalized by the dearth of other Black institutions, and mobilized by the past, present, and future condition of the Black community.

The Black Church has long been recognized as the heart, pulse, and drum of the African-American community. In fact, some argue that it is the

---

1. See Lincoln and Mamiya, *Black Church in the African American Experience*.
2. See Savage, *Your Spirits Walk Among Us*.

INTRODUCTION

community.³ Throughout the struggles of Blacks in this nation, the Black Church has been an evolutionary fixture and a revolutionary foundation for the Black community. From harnessing hope during slavery to providing leadership during the civil rights movement, the narrative of the Black Church sprouts from the survival and liberation of individuals in an enslaved and segregated American society. This narrative of the Black Church does several things relative to civil society: one, documents its involvement in, and interaction with, the public sphere; two, validates its viability as a contemporary mediating institution; three, creates space for dialogue, deliberation, and discourse; and four, marks its potentiality as an agent of change.

While the earliest Black churches differed in terms of denominational identities, systems of polity, doctrinal beliefs, and practices, this did not obscure their fundamental, consensus agreement concerning the need to challenge the status quo—hence, the term *Black Church*. The Black Church was born into a culture that did not separate private devotion from public duty. Invariably, this meant that the church had to move beyond the strictly spiritual and ecclesiastical to promote positive change in the social, economic, and political aspects of life.⁴ When referring to the Black Church as "an all-comprehending institution", Carter G. Woodson surmised:

> The Negro church touches almost every ramification of the life of the Negro. As stated elsewhere, the Negro church, in the absence of other agencies to assume such responsibilities, has had to do more than its duty in taking care of the general interests of the race. A definitive history of the Negro church, therefore, would leave practically no phase of the history of the Negro in America untouched. All efforts of the Negro in things economic, educational and political have branched out of or connected in some way with the rise and development of the Negro Church.⁵

Because of this, the Black Church has no challenger as the cultural womb of the Black community and it has only been recently that scholars of African-American history, culture, and theology have begun to recognize its unique and distinctive traditional aspects not as simply replications of a dominant culture.⁶ In many instances, most community anchors—schools, stores, restaurants—were birthed by the Black Church through its membership, and

3. See Mitchell, *Black Church Beginnings*.
4. See Baldwin's "Revisiting the 'All-Comprehending Institution.'"
5. See Woodson, "The Negro Church, an All-Comprehending Institution."
6. See Lincoln and Mamiya, *The Black Church in the African-American Experience*.

as a result, the Black Church became a middle-ground between individuals and social institutions, the realm commonly referred to as "civic."

Christian ethicist and theologian Gary Simpson argues that the notion of representation in "representative publicness" does not refer to an assembly of delegates who represent ordinary people, but rather highlights and accentuates the gulf in status between the elite and the commoner.[7] While civic literature broadly holds that participating in institutions is important to the development of skills and trust in individual citizens,[8] and that these skills and trust can then be translated into the type of social skill and trust that are necessary for democratic processes and governance, implicit and explicit challenges arise when applying traditional civic literature to the Black Church. Embedded in a sizable part of this literature is the assumption that participation in voluntary associations such as churches serves to reinforce the social order—however disproportionate, dysfunctional, and discriminatory.[9] Yet, the Black Church has historically carved out "free spaces" to both cultivate civic loyalty as well as inculcate civil disobedience. Frederick Harris refers to this ability, to both reinforce civic loyalty as well as challenge inequality and inequity, as "an oppositional civic culture."[10] He further explains that the Black Church serves as a source of civic culture by providing Blacks the opportunity to develop positive orientations toward the civic order. The same institution, however, also provides the Black community with resources and dispositions to challenge its marginality.[11]

In an accommodative role, the Black Church served as the major cultural broker of norms, values, and expectations, thus the subsequent view as a mediating structure and its becoming a network of support.[12] In a role of resistance, the Black Church functioned as the primary source for affirming cultural heritage to withstand mainstream pressures of conformity and compliance, and thus, becoming a vehicle for social change.[13] Operating in this dialectic, one can easily draw the conclusion that the Black community, both historically and at present, cannot be understood apart

---

7. See Simpson, *Critical Social Theory*.
8. See Coleman, *Foundations of Social Theory*.
9. See Calhoun-Brown's "What A Fellowship."
10. See Harris, *Something Within*.
11. Ibid.
12. Term introduced in Berger and Neuhaus, *To Empower People*. See Eberly, *The Essential Civil Society Reader*.
13. See Franklin, *Crisis in the Village*.

from the Black Church which recognizes and serves the most vital personal interests of the individual without abandoning or avoiding the interests of the collective to which it is attached.[14] Despite the widely held justification of slavery as a means of spreading the gospel, the economic profitability of slaves, not their Christianization, held top priority in mission work.[15] Consequently, mission in the Black Church has always focused on freedom. While physical and political freedoms were necessary first steps, freedom, in its entirety, meant the assault on any inhibiting factors or conditions which precluded certain individuals from the inalienable rights promised within the Constitution.

Under the oppressive conditions that forced Blacks to create alternate social structures, a socially-conscious Black Church developed in the midst of oppression, segregation, and marginalization. In other words, in a racist context that did not allow for equality or equity, to either join mainstream voluntary organizations or access resources to establish any civic institutions, the only widely accessible communal associations for the Black community was the Black Church. The unique circumstances, in which the Black Church emerged, as well as the cultural and societal context in which it operates, give it a dualistic positioning that can either reinforce social order, or challenge this order—a historic duality that has long been its tradition.

Social Gospel & Community Implications

In chronological context, the social gospel can be understood as a transitional phase of Christian social thought, a sub-movement within religious liberalism, "with a certain view of man and history governing its rationale."[16] As early as 1910 within the Protestant Christian movement, the social gospel emphasized an application of Christian principles to society's problems, which prior to this had been unvoiced amid the growing problems of industrial society. Given this context, its moral message consisted almost exclusively in applications, mild or severe, of the idea that the doctrine of laissez faire required Christian modifications.[17]

---

14. See Eberly, *The Essential Civil Society Reader*.
15. See Raboteau, *Slave Religion*.
16. Ahlstrom, *A Religious History of the American People*.
17. Ibid.

The initial fervor and fire of the Social Gospel movement argued against capitalism and individualism while seeking to apply Christian ethics to current social ills, motivated by a concern for finding societal truth and justice. In a time when many mainline Protestant churches were largely allied with the social and political establishment, in effect supporting systemic injustice and institutional oppression, the connection of social issues to church mission was a novelty. Far from biblical radicalism however, the Social Gospel's basic political thrust is illustrated by what historian Sydney Ahlstrom claims was its gradual progression from the abstract moral protest to a specific critique of American economic institutions,[18] obligating followers of Christ to act to improve the conditions affecting God's people.

The nature of the Black Church is constituted and maintained through its communitarian sensibilities. In other words, the essence of the Black Church is community, which moves beyond the European Enlightenment framework of individualism. The individual is part of the whole, individual identity flows from corporate experience, never in isolation from it; community defines who one becomes, and who one becomes, in turn, shapes the community. The Black Church can be characterized as a dialectic between communal and independent; *communal* referring to the historic tradition of Black churches being involved in all aspects of members' lives, and *independent* meaning removed from the concerns and control of the larger, White society. As a result, the Black Church has been able to play a defining civic role due in part to its formal institutional character, but also because of its informal social nature that has provided a context for action and construct for influence. In the past, during periods of severe and sustained crises in Black communities, individuals would turn to the Black Church for guidance, support, and leadership. In turn, the Black Church would respond not within the biblical boundary of pietistic mission where the primary focus was spiritual practices to guide God's children, but beyond such ecclesial understandings to instead engage the ethical and moral implications of systemic practices in order to address the social conditions affecting the Black community.

The Functional Drift

Throughout the social changes that Black Americans have undergone since the 1960s, the Black Church's minimized prophetic impulse has been

18. Ibid.

accompanied by a fully American cultural emphasis on individual, to the exclusion of community. When W.E.B. DuBois coined the term "double-consciousness," he referred to the struggle of Blacks to navigate between two incompatible cultural identities—Black and American. In this particular instance, maintaining cultural roots as a means of preserving identity and building community has been a key task of the Black Church. This task involves a constant interplay "between the pain of oppression and the promise of liberation found in the Bible, on one hand, and a similar existence experienced" today on the other.[19] This dichotomy becomes more profound as the internal culture of the Black Church begins to adopt mainstream characteristics—achievement, success, and status—just to name a few. Within the culture of the Black Church are the preserved doctrines of salvation and reconciliation of humanity envisioned in the Kingdom of God as the primary characteristics of its ecclesial self-image. However, the ideology of American individualism belies salvation and reconciliation, exacerbating an existing and growing bifurcation within the Black community. Many among the disadvantaged Black classes greatly distrust the actions and interests not only of the Black middle-and upper-classes, but of the Black Church as well.[20] Individualism in the Black Church is a microcosm of the American pursuit of personal gain, marking a major disruption of corporate identity and communal responsibility, and increasing amid the struggles for socioeconomic advancement conditioned by American individualism.[21] The presence and prominence of individualism within the Black Church subverts mutuality between it and the community, contributing to a fragmentation of the larger Black community, and resulting in the displacement of the Black Church and its identification with the Black community.

The legitimacy of any organization is its ability to transform subjective reality to sustain its relationality. Otherwise a redefining and reinterpreting of said reality and relationality become disrupted.[22] Curtailed civic engagement is a clear reflection of this disruption. The civic engagement of the Black Church has drifted from prophetic radicalism to pragmatic accommodationism, as termed by public theologian Robert Franklin, and represents a functional challenge to the Black Church to sustain a contemporary,

19. Hopkins, *Heart and Head*, 7.
20. Blackwell, *The Black Community*, 96.
21. Andrews, *Practical Theology for Black Churches*, 60.
22. Ibid., 64.

social purpose while simultaneously maintaining a historical, social premise. Or in other words, to be the "communicator of culture and translator of Christianity," clarifying and connecting aspects of ministry to the Black experience.[23]

According to Franklin, prophetic radicalism employs a confrontation and negotiation method aimed at evoking a crisis, attracting attention, and building support for dramatic social, cultural, and political change, while pragmatic accommodationism seeks to effect change through a cooperation and compromise strategy with the status quo.[24] A functional drift occurs when the Black Church, which has always served as the Black "culture center," begins to adopt the premises and practices of its dominant social predicament, specifically American individualism.

Since the 1960s, social conditions have led to extended reflections from Black theologians on what it means to claim a religious faith and be Black in America.[25] Such reflection is critical because identity, culture, and relationships became changing variables as Black strivings for middle-class position and acceptability in the dominant culture created great distance between the Black Church and its intended audience. Just as Congregationalists and Episcopalians lost touch with their constituencies in the eighteenth-century, the Black Church's ineffectiveness is clearly marked by its lack of relationship with the larger Black community—the middle-and upper-classes of the Black community feel no sense of connection to the historic Black Church, while the lower-class has no sentiment of companionship. Additionally, the perceived improved social, economic, and political standing of Blacks has not only affected the expectation of the Black Church, but in the midst of social ferment and crises in the Black community, has led to a less prophetic Black Church that does little to critique, challenge, or change institutional and systemic injustices.

The thought that an individual can achieve in spite of social constrictions becomes favored, President Barack Obama as a prime example, thus ignoring the presence, prevalence, and persistence of systemic inequities and social injustices. Unfortunately, in their effort to become "mainstream,"[26]

---

23. See Conyers Jr., *Black Cultures and Race Relations* and Franklin, *Another Day's Journey*.

24. Franklin, *Another Day's Journey*, 51.

25. See West, *Prophetic Fragments* and Anderson, *Beyond Ontological Blackness*..

26. Mainstream being defined as institutional assimilation to achieve social acceptance of the dominant culture in such a way that the original fiber, foundation, and function of the institution is misplaced, ignored, and/or compromised.

INTRODUCTION

many churches become either willing partners in the sins of society, or at least partners by neglect, and thereby eschew their prophetic commission.[27] Ironically, such a position is only possible after the Black Church's prophetic engagement during periods of slavery, segregation, dehumanization, and disenfranchisement. So, how can the Black Church socially reposition itself now without compromising its prophetic identity?

This Book

This project is an attempt to understand, from the pulpit, pew and community, the prophetic nature of the Black Church. The inquiry targeted the social gospel dimensions of the historic Black Church. This investigation contributes to existing literature in two primary ways. First, it underscores the role, often not addressed in academic literature that pastoral leaders can play, have played, and do play in the practice of "public theology."[28] Second, it advances previous research by empirically delineating some of the perspectives and practices performed by pastors and churches that lend themselves to civic engagement. The third feature is that of the Black Church as a form of American religious expression. While it ought to be viewed as part of a mainstream heritage, it tends "to be understood as marginal and exotic addenda."[29] Couple this understanding with what George Hunsberger identifies as "significant trajectories" that exist to open fruitful conversation between missiology and public theology, and the potential significance of this study unveils larger implications: first, it delves into the social, political, and ecclesial contributions of the Black Church relative to civic engagement—while the prevailing biblical and field scholarship typically give a mainline, White perspective, this research broadens the scholarly wisdom to consider and include a specific minority and ethnic perspective; second, this research takes into account the holistic effects of civil rights achievement and the impact of American individualism on the development of civil rights; and third, this undertaking could provide options for reframing civic engagement not only by the Black Church, but also by the field of missional ecclesiology.

The Bible enabled the constitution of a new Black person. Frederick Douglass received this revelation about the transformative power of the

27. See Andrews, *Practical Theology for Black Churches*.
28. See Hunsberger's "The Missional Voice and Posture of Public Theologizing."
29. Franklin's "The Safest Place on Earth."

xvii

INTRODUCTION

inspired text, in part, from overhearing his master's objections to providing Douglass reading instruction: "If he learns to read the Bible," his master said, "it will forever unfit him to be a slave."[30] For Douglass, this statement struck like a bolt of lightning from heaven, converting his old confused self into a participatory practitioner bent on emancipation. His discovery of a new network—connecting newfound access to profound reality—removed Douglass from the power of his master and propelled him into a new space, metaphorically and literally. Thus, in this example, an enslaved Black person recreated self and world by receiving and perceiving imposed dynamics, then transforming and transposing them for his or her own liberation—thereby fusing an experiential horizon with that of potential. What enslaved religious Blacks called secret meetings, commonly termed "invisible institution," reflected the location out of which a future Black theology of liberation emerged.

In chapter 1, I identify a working definition of missional ecclesiology by isolating the terms. The isolation is not meant to devalue the collective, but rather to highlight the cultural significance of each as stand-alone theological constructs. I argue that the manner in which different cultures engage the collective term is critically determined by how those particular cultures interpret them individually. This constructive approach then seeks to associate how the conditions under which the Black Church began significantly impacted the purpose it assumed moving forward.

Chapter 2 provides a theological framework that highlights the Black spiritual approach that connects other-worldly belief with this-worldly action. On one hand, Black identity had been dictated by a system designed to dehumanize enslaved Blacks and sever any spiritual premise from liberative practice. On the other, proper Christian understanding demanded the combining of Godly principles with earthly practice, especially as it pertained to the liberation of an oppressed people. With constant appeal to, and affirmation from, the biblical narrative, Blacks approached social conditions as part of, not apart from, their Christian faith. This prophetic engagement was championed by church leaders who argued for a holistic approach to freedom—one that thrust social conditions, economic policies, and political practices into theological discourse.

I begin chapter 3 with an overview of several theories related to the effects of the Black Church—does the Black Church act as a stimulant which inspires civic engagement, or as an opiate inspiring no activity

30. See Douglass, *Life and Times of Frederick Douglass*.

whatsoever. By outlining several perspectives, chapter four crystallizes two main themes—pragmatic accommodationism and prophetic radicalism—that moves the exploration forward by helping to characterize the role of pastoral leadership. As I interject the multidimensional and multifunctional aspects of the Black Church and pastoral leadership, the characterization is then placed in conversation with Hans-George Gadamer's 'fusion of horizon' theory to capture the civic possibilities of the Black Church. The characterization process culminates in the examination of leadership theory through the lens of the Black Church—specifically, leadership definition, change theory, and networked organizational concepts—thereby making the case that evolved leadership and adaptable organizational approaches are both required if the Black Church is to relevantly move forward.

Chapter 4 documents the combined effects of pastoral leadership, historical understanding, social awareness, and biblical comprehension. Maintaining consistency with earlier theological and theoretical perspectives, this chapter begins to unfold how the Black Church has travailed on a "connect vs. disconnect" paradigm and utilizes the three theoretical impulses identified in chapter 4 to help shape the qualitative and quantitative findings. I close this chapter by bringing in Walter Brueggemann's idea of prophetic ministry and its corrective, radical approach to dominant culture.

The Black Church, it seems, finds its roots in the prophetic approach but presently appears to run away from dutiful praxis. I interpret this theological opportunity as the Black Church's missional ecclesiological moment, and in chapter 5, highlight three areas where it can effectively make the most of this opportunity: knowledge and negotiation of social power dynamics, reconciliatory role of education for academia and ecclesia, and finally, the pursuit of effective civic partnerships.

Chapter One

Setting the Stage

Introduction

WHY IS STAYING WITHIN the city gates, confines of one's community, or organizational silos so natural and preferable? A sociological response could be that what is known breeds a certain level of security and comfort, but a spiritual reply would question whether earthly security and comfort should be goals of the sojourner. This has been the question at the center of the missional conversation. With either response, an important understanding for the church is its dual nature: social and spiritual—the church situated in a social context with a spiritual calling. And, as such, its missional ecclesiology has to address and engage the dynamics, factors, and qualities of its context if it is to be faithful to its calling.

In this chapter, I will attempt to frame the missional conversation from a biblical perspective touching on both Old and New Testament narratives. This intent is to transition into a "public" defining of ecclesial practices and social characteristics such as the Black Church's reconstitution of mission and a macro/micro comprehension of culture. Revisiting Black Church beginnings, specifically the slave period, I begin to frame how mission in a Black context integrates liberation from, and participation in, the social systems and structures that not only shaped its culture, but were once prohibited. My aim here is to point out that in order for missional ecclesiology to be biblically-reflective and spiritually-effective, it needs to be contextually-informed.

The Future Horizon for a Prophetic Tradition

Framing Conversation

A careful analysis of the biblical story reveals dialectic between centripetal and centrifugal forces concerning mission. A scan of Jewish history in the Old Testament uncovers flight from and absorption of the secular, a concern for self-identity and responsible (or irresponsible!) interaction with one's environment, elect status as God's chosen people as well as a humble awareness of one's solidarity with humanity entirely.[1] A screening of the New Testament discovers the fundamental aspects of Jesus' confined ministry that sought to challenge and restore the community of Israel, and how they became an inspiration and source for post-Easter universal mission of community—representing multiple ways in which members of the Christian community reflected on their missionary purpose and its relationship to the personhood of Jesus and the history of Israel.[2]

Arguing against an operational ecclesiology that is more instrumental in character, the missional church conversation has reintroduced a discussion about the very nature, or essence, of the church.[3] This conversation no longer understands "being missionary" primarily in functional terms, as something the church *does*, but rather in terms of something the church *is*, as something related to its nature—representing a change that places ecclesiology more front and center.[4] In this regard, the focus shifts toward the world as the horizon for understanding the work of God, and that redemptive work as the basis for understanding both the nature and purpose of the church,[5] replacing the operational ecclesiology, characterized by an organizational self-understanding around a purposive intent, with an ecclesiology that comprehends the church as being created by the Spirit and, in nature, missionary.

Initially, the missional church conversation concentrated on the sending nature of the triune, missionary God: God the Father sends Jesus the Son who then sends the Holy Spirit, who in turn sends the church to the world. This conversation introduces two streams of understanding God's work in the world. First, the missio Dei—God has a mission within all of creation; and second, God has brought redemption to bear on all of life

---

1. Senior and Stuhlmueller, *The Biblical Foundations for Mission*, 316.
2. Ibid.
3. Van Gelder, *The Missional Church & Denominations*, 42.
4. Ibid.
5. Ibid., 43.

within creation through the life, death, and resurrection of Jesus Christ.[6] In an attempt to recover the relational nature of the Triune God, the missional church conversation has more recently adopted somewhat of a retrieval of trinitarian theology where God seeks to bring to His kingdom, "the redemptive reign of God in Christ, to bear on every dimension of life within the entire world" so His larger creation purposes can be fulfilled.[7] This relational dimension is grounded in the fundamental bridging of social context and spiritual calling.

Ecclesial Aspect

Public is a word that resides at every turn in the missional ecclesiology conversation. The word *ekklesia* itself emanates from the idea of a civic meeting as does its Hebrew counterpart *qahal*, which refers to a deliberative assembly of the body politic. Public is associated with the New Testament word *kerygma* and its verbal vicissitudes. Usually translated "preaching," it is far removed from what we now label preaching. According to George Hunsberger,

> its meaning field has to do with the function of the "herald," the news announcement by the official spokesvoice of one in power or authority. The public broadcast of the news, the "*public*ation" of it, is the form of witness the New Testament describes.[8]

Once clear that the church is not simply an organization based on membership, but a body of people bounded by a mission—settling the fact of *who* we are—then *where* we are is not the building on the corner, or the ivory institution on the hill, but people pressed into the fabric of life, living it out in the social context and public dimensions shared by others.[9] Civic engagement then becomes the welcomed outcome of this "sharing" because it is within such a public society that individuals and institutions learn to cultivate the virtues of citizenship.

As associated, "connected critics,"[10] individuals and institutions committed to fundamental, communal ideas can functionally observe the

---

6. Ibid.
7. Ibid., 44.
8. Hunsberger, "The Missional Voice and Posture of Public Theologizing," 17.
9. Ibid., 18
10. Thiemann, *Religion in Public Life: A Dilemma for Democracy*, 152.

shortcomings of a public society while engaging and immanently critiquing the very same enterprise. Critical social theorist Max Horkheimer based his theory of society on the notion of an "immanent critique," arguing that normative rational ideas, which simultaneously serve to critically evaluate as well as redesign and rebuild a different society, are themselves present within a given social system. He explains: "Immanent critique summons the existent [society], in its historical context, with the claim of its conceptual principles, in order to criticize the relation between the two and thus transcend them."[11]

In succession, immanent critique restates and redefines the "norms and ideals that have been forgotten or repressed, usually because they inconvenience a social class or social arrangement."[12] It can then serve as a contemporary conscience[13] that weaves together public opinion and public power, highlighting Simpson's point that "those who bear especially the impoverishing, dispossessing consequences of economic or democratic policy, or of any decision venue, must be full participants with effective voice in the decision-making bodies, processes, and procedures.[14] This represents a "democratic solidarity and publicity"[15] that addresses the crucial question of who discerns, deliberates, and decides by following what he terms "the participatory golden rule"—decision-makers must be consequence-takers, and consequence-takers must be decision-makers.[16]

---

11. Simpson, *Critical Social Theory*, 56.

12. Ibid., 127.

13. Philosopher Joseph Butler believed that the most fundamental aspect of human nature is the conscience which he defines as the reflective or rational faculty which discerns the moral characteristics of actions. For Butler, conscience is a type of moral reason which distinguishes right from wrong.

14. See Simpson, "God in Global Society."

15. Solidarity being a key condition for developing moral wisdom thereby playing a constitutive role in a publicly-effective moral epistemology allowing critical issues to be identified, distilled, and framed—manifesting itself through proposals, programs, and practices for moral and cultural formation, or critical reformation. Publicity takes what has been critically-identified, morally-framed and formed, and programmatically-proposed and makes that fully public—meaning, in a transparent and accessible manner, publicity connects what it discovers concerning the social condition to the systems of power that can cause and effect change.

16. See Simpson, "God in Global Society."

Culture Clash

Lesslie Newbigin straightforwardly asserts that neither at the beginning, nor at any subsequent time, is there or can there be a gospel that is not embodied in a cultural condition.[17] The early focus of the diaspora communities was on serving the religious needs of the people while preserving the cultural identity of their spirituality. So, while missionaries and "enlightened" Christians professed a concern for the spiritual well-being of indigenous peoples, they were primarily shaped by their cultural superiority complexes as most understood "civilizing" and "evangelizing" to go hand-in-hand.[18] This began to create tension around the purpose of, and premise behind, mission as the political and economic forces of colonialism, manifest destiny, and imperialism reflected and reinforced the feelings of religious and human superiority, which quite naturally led to perceived indigenous cultural inferiority. The mission came out of a context that assumed the supremacy of Western culture and "the White Man's Religion," that is, Christianity, and as a result, established a tension regarding the overall aim of mission, begging the question: How can Christian community be realized if human and cultural equity are not recognized?

Christians have always used the Bible as the primary guide for missional activity. In doing so, they have mined those rich resources in a myriad of ways and for multiple reasons: personal, seeking inspiration to rekindle and guide missionary motivation; practical, to address specific problems or to underwrite certain strategies; and structural, usage of scripture as a blueprint for missionary activity and criteria for the establishment of the Christian community.[19]

However, careful use of biblical scholarship has unmasked a more radical, transforming and equitable biblical message, one "which reflects the breadth and diversity of perspectives in the Scriptures themselves."[20] Missional ecclesiology should, therefore, challenge churches to be intentional about their unique social potential within their specific cultural contexts. In this way, Western culture, incubated by the premises of colonialism, manifest destiny, and imperialism, agrees with indigenous culture inculcated by an eschatological hope that sustained generations through the very same

---

17. See Newbigin, *Foolishness to the Greeks.*
18. Bevans and Schroeder, *Constants in Context*, 230.
19. Senior and Stuhlmueller, *The Biblical Foundations for Mission*, Foreword.
20. Guder, *Missional Church*, 11.

practices of colonialism, manifest destiny, and imperialism.[21] Hope in God's coming eschatological freedom sustained suffering people who were seeking to establish freedom on earth even though it had not yet been achieved in their the level of human standing.[22] The most significant circumstances that shaped indigenous culture were dehumanization, degradation, and the need for a liberating message amidst oppression. This reality provided the practical challenge to develop mission that was not only responsible in a faithful Christian concept, but respectful in a functional cultural context as well. This juxtaposition shifted the understanding of mission from *"with"* to *"of"*, as *"with"* often carries paternalistic overtones that infantilize the other, thereby suppressing the participatory and communicative spirit of freedom, equality, mutuality, and solidarity connoted by *"of."*[23]

Black Culture/Church Reconstitution of Mission

To maintain their destined and divine power, White masters prohibited Black slaves from learning to read, particularly the Bible. Although legally restricted, Black chattel subverted this mechanism of power by appropriating and claiming the sacred narrative from their dehumanized vantage as those at the bottom of the social, economic, and political economy. This seizure of power helped the slaves constitute themselves as human beings created in the image of Christ, while reconstituting mission that has as its telos, its inner aim, an apostolic rationale. That is to say, it is not simply called to follow Christ in a generic sense, but rather to steward in a specific service, in a particular context, or, as Hunsberger argues, to recognize Jesus to *be* the truth, and be intent—in forms of thinking, speaking, and acting—on being *true* to that understanding.[24] *That* mission, publicly-performed, provides a theological framework through which private beliefs can be *transformed* into public consciousness, public consciousness *transferred* into prophetic action, and prophetic action *translated* into the public good.

---

21. After the Civil War, the Reconstruction Period began and the economic life of the South, which was based on free slave labor, had to be restored. The most striking aspect of the post-war circumstance was that the United States Congress passed the 14th Amendment in 1866, which made former slaves citizens, and extended to them equal protection under the law and protection against state interference with their life, liberty, and property.

22. See Freedman, *Upon This Rock*.

23. See Simpson, "God in Global Society."

24. Hunsberger, "The Missional Voice and Posture of Public Theologizing," 22.

The reconstitution of mission created a syncretized religion that implicitly recognized culture and explicitly rhetoricized Christianity, harmonizing contextual placement and Christian purpose. The result was not only in a missional salvific process, but a prophetic ecclesial practice as well, of which Lawrence Jones writes:

> The significance of a religious institution cannot be calibrated solely in terms of the number of conversions it records, in the growth of its membership, or in other measurements utilized by ecclesiastical bodies. The statistical indices inevitably reflect, to some degree, perceptions of the seriousness of the church's commitment to enhancing the quality of life in the community in which it is located. Favorable perceptions invariably result in church growth. But faithfulness to the Christian Gospel, which they proclaim, requires gathered communities of faith to be involved in the changing panorama of political, economic, social, demographic, educational and cultural realities in which persons live out their lives.[25]

This publicly engaged missional ecclesiology emerged from a culture of reasoning, revolution, and reform that became the life and legacy of the Black Church—liberating activity. With the resources of this religious tradition, Black Church identity reflected God's vision for the world. It is an identity deriving from an encounter with God in the midst of pains and struggles of the dehumanized that refused to accept despair as a logical consequence of oppression. Kathryn Tanner suggests that culture is not primarily located in the intellectual or spiritual achievements of the community, but rather refers to the whole social practice of meaningful action and more specifically to the meaning dimension of such action and how it suffuses the whole way of life.[26] Such a cultural approach sets the table for a public church dimension of missional ecclesiology that engages the plurality of a social context, and thereby provides an inclusive way to move forward, engage systems, and challenge structures while creating a new paradigm for collaboration, integration and interrogation.

---

25. Billingsley, *Mighty Like a River*, Foreword.
26. Tanner, *Theories of Culture*, 70.

Black Church Beginnings

It is no accident that Black spokespersons of the nineteenth century popularized the idea that the history of Black religion begins neither among the slaves of pious Whites in New England and Virginia, nor on the plantations of South Carolina and Georgia, but in Africa.[27] As Albert J. Raboteau argues, "Thousands of Africans from diverse cultures and religious traditions, forcibly transported to America as slaves, retained many African customs even as they converted to Christianity."[28] Thus, any investigation of the historic Black Church, with its inherent propensity for radical social and political action, should begin appropriately addressing the connection to Africa and African Diaspora.

The gospel first appeared in Africa in the Upper Nile Valley where a man of Ethiopia, a eunuch named Judich[29] of great authority under Candace the queen of the Ethiopians, was baptized between Jerusalem and Gaza by Philip, the Evangelist.[30] Blacks from Africa served in the Roman army in the first years of the Christian era, and many, like St. Maurice,[31] converted to Christianity. Over time, the strikingly African character of early Ethiopian Christianity became apparent. One account records,

> They sing the Psalms of David of which as well as other parts of the Holy Scriptures, they have a very exact translation in their own language ... The instruments of music[k] made use of in their rites of worship, are little drums, which they hang about their necks, and beat with both hands ... They begin their consort by stamping their feet on the ground, and playing gently on their instruments, but when they heated themselves by degrees, they leave off drumming and fall into leaping, dancing, and clapping their hands at the same time straining their voices to their utmost pitch, till at length they have no regard either to the tune, or the pauses, and seem rather a riotous, than a religious assembly.[32]

---

27. Wilmore, *Black Religion and Black Radicalism*, 2.
28. Raboteau, *Canaan Land*, ix.
29. See Eusebius of Caesarea, *Ecclesiastical History*, II, 1, 13.
30. Acts 8:26–40
31. St. Maurice was a Black African general who, while stationed in Switzerland during the 3rd century, refused to lead his legion against the Bagaudae after discovering that the White Gallic tribesmen were Christian. Because of this insubordination and refusal to sacrifice to pagan gods, Maurice and his men were executed by Augustus Maximilian.
32. Groves, *The Planting of Christianity in Africa*, 141–42.

With the origination, continuation, and proliferation of the transatlantic slave trade (initially begun by the Portuguese, then accompanied and rivaled by the British), the plantation colonies of the Americas gave birth to an integrated Christianity that coupled the social condition and cultural practices of the African slave. Under the circumstances, the integrated Christianity functioned as a survival kit, containing rules, values, and modes of action that helped individuals as well as a community cope with the realities of their existence. Certainly, the realities of this world for the slave warranted a vastly different type of religion than that for the slaveowner, leading to what Gayraud Wilmore labels "African American (or Black) religion."[33]

The "Invisible Institution"

Slavery was already a practice among some West African populations, but Arab slave traders first introduced African slaves into Europe, on a significant scale, by way of Spain and Portugal in 1502.[34] Initially, the British colonies permitted a different practice: a seven-year term of service after which the bonded person was to be freed and awarded land to sustain himself—indentured servitude. This was based on an Old Testament practice meant to wean the Israelites, newly freed from slavery themselves, away from the practice of slavery entirely.[35] Therefore, poor British people voluntarily entered into indentured servitude hoping to find higher economic standing in the New World at the conclusion of their service. This was the circumstance in which African "slaves" were procured from the Spanish and Portuguese and brought into indentured servitude. Consequently, the first Africans in English America were not "slaves" at all, but on the contrary, arrived on the same socioeconomic terms as many English and Irish settlers.[36]

Colonists quickly discovered that it was economically advantageous to exploit African versus European servants. If they were, for example, to oppress British subjects by extending their term of service or refusing proper compensation at the end, the servants could appeal to the king for assistance. African servants, however, had no structure or entity with whom to appeal resulting in the imported exploitation of African slave

---

33. Wilmore, *Black Religion and Black Radicalism*, 22.
34. Anstey, *The Atlantic Slave Trade and British Abolition, 1760–1810*.
35. Leviticus 25:39–43; Deuteronomy 15:12–18
36. Bennett Jr., *Before the Mayflower*.

labor into British territory. This served as the economic premise behind the social construction of race,[37] which was simply an ideology created to justify colonial practices and economic exploitation while relieving European consciences.[38] According to Michael Battle:

> Racial identity became associated with the people of Europe, who sought to colonize the world. In particular, white bodies and white minds sought to dominate black bodies and black minds. Such domination became the fabric of the Enlightenment worldview that created theological and legal boundaries of inclusion and exclusion.[39]

Theologically, the White interpretation of Christianity effectively divested the slave of any concern about freedom. Marked with inconsistencies, the doctrinal gulf between the allegation of the all-powerful God of the Whites who could care so much about eternal salvation and yet remain indifferent and silent about existential conditions left the slave skeptical and wanting. Operating from a hermeneutic of suspicion, the slaves adopted the outward appearance of White Christian conversion, but took from it only what proved efficacious for easing the burden of bondage. Wilmore asserts:

> All of its deficiencies and excesses notwithstanding, the religion that the slaves practiced was their own. It was unmistakably the religion of an oppressed, but not entirely conquered, people. It had, of course, common features with Euro-American Protestantism and, in the French-speaking and Spanish-speaking Caribbean, with Roman Catholicism. But it was not forged in the drawing rooms of the elegant mansions of Virginia and South Carolina, or in the segregated galleries of the northern churches. It was born out of the experience of being black and understanding blackness to be somehow connected with being held in bondage and needing to be free.

Amidst these openly hostile practices, hidden communal practices began to take shape. As soon as enough Africans were settled in a single location, they readily recalled and shared the commonalities of their African religious traditions and adapted their already similar worship practices. Records of their being forbidden to gather clearly establish the fact that, regardless of the variety of tribal backgrounds on any given plantation, they

---

37. López, *White by Law*.
38. Lincoln, *Race, Religion, and the Continuing American Dilemma*.
39. Battle, *The Black Church in America*, 28.

did gather and devoutly engage in an African style of common worship.[40] Peter Randolph recounts,

> slaves yearned for greater spiritual refreshing in their communal meetings and often stole away to Jesus by assembling in quarters, swamps, and "hush harbors." There they could hold meetings with preachers of their own. There they consoled one another, prayed, sang, and joined in ritual movement patterned after the African "ring-shout."[41]

This underground evolution developed despite slave codes that were enacted to curb disorderly conduct and profaning of the Sabbath. The "invisible institution" emerged because Black slaves felt the compelling need to worship and serve God, not out of a particular revelatory experience or principle that overshadowed their social and physical conditions, but based on the notion of a God who was personally involved in His creation and on "an invisible institution," as Battle articulates, "in which Africans inculturated Christianity in such a way as to facilitate survival throughout slavery."[42]

The Slave Quandary

Contained within this "invisible institution," a quandary emerged between the passive and active expectations of freedom. Was it incumbent upon the slave to "rest in the Lord, and wait patiently"[43] for deliverance, or, should the slave "proclaim liberty to the captives, and the opening of the prison to those who are bound?"[44] Thus, the slave quandary became a question of how to confront the existential evil—endure or survive bondage until God brings forth a new age of freedom into reality, or take the initiative to escape or overthrow the present practice of injustice. Survival did not depend on a passive and impotent acceptance of circumstance. In fact, for the slave it took the form of proactive participation in the redemptive activity of God, despite the deliberate distortion of Christian doctrine and stringent restrictions upon religious activity. A distinctive African American form of

---

40. Chenu, *The Trouble I've Seen*, 49.
41. Randolph's "Plantation Churches."
42. Battle, *The Black Church in America*, 57.
43. Psalm 37:7
44. Isaiah 61:1

Christianity slowly took root, one that contained a definite moral judgment against slavery and clearly legitimized resistance to injustice.[45]

As early as 1732, in a message to the Virginia House of Burgesses, Governor Drysdale remarked on the difficulty the colony was having in detecting and punishing slave insurrections. That year the legislature passed new laws concerning the control of slaves because the regulations then in effect were "found insufficient to restrain their tumultuous and unlawful meetings, or to punish the secret plots and conspiracies carried amongst them."[46] According to Wilmore,

> [T]hese "tumultuous and unlawful meetings" were, in all probability, religious meetings where the emotions of the slaves, whipped to a frenzy by a preacher, rose to such an intensity that they were extremely vulnerable to an appeal, in the context of a sermon or prayer, to throw off their chains in an uprising.[47]

These clandestine gatherings became the spark that ignited flames of revolt, heightening the suspicion that religion was a primary factor in slave uprisings. Governor John Floyd expressed the opinion that the spirit of insubordination and insurrection among the slaves had its origins in the belief that God was no respecter of persons, meaning that the Black man was as good as the White and "that the white people rebelled against England to obtain freedom, so have blacks a right to do so."[48] For the "invisible institution," God was thus simultaneously transcendent and immanent, and upon this element was pinned its theology of hope.

The Appropriation of Scripture

The implications of liberation contained in the biblical narrative, basic to the New Testament and Reformation theology, were readily, and had no difficulty being, recalled by the leaders of America's War of Independence. Such implications were, however, assiduously avoided when conveyed to slaves. Rather, Christian theology and ethics were reduced to their most simplistic and innocuous affirmations, a favorite being, "Servants, be obedient to them that are your masters according to the flesh, with fear and trembling,

---

45. Wilmore, *Black Religion and Black Radicalism*, 48.
46. Aptheker, *American Negro Slave Revolts*, 162.
47. Wilmore, *Black Religion and Black Radicalism*, 54.
48. Aptheker, *American Negro Slave Revolts*, 106–7.

in singleness of your heart, as unto Christ."[49] Despite the deliberate distortion of Christian doctrine and stringent restrictions upon religious activity, Africans in America began to appropriate Scripture and to shape a distinctive, contextually-relevant slave religion. Uneducated by Western standards, but far from ignorant, the slave began to practice a Christianity that incorporated a mystical sense of prophecy and divine intervention that "assured a measure of self-determination and continuity with the past, by diverting certain biblical and theological conceptions of Christianity into structures of belief and practice that more adequately served the needs of the slaves."[50]

A striking distinction of the slave religion was the slaves' thorough knowledge of Scripture. The spirituals, writings, and sermons of the time express a special affinity to the people of the Old Testament. The God of Israel was the Lord of hosts, the God of battles who swept His enemies before the faces of His chosen people. The great prophets, who had fought against the idolatry, hypocrisy, and social injustices, perfectly suited the religious sentiment of the slaves. But preeminent relevance for slaves, "as many of the most famous spirituals bear witness, was found in the story of Exodus."[51] The bondage of the Hebrews, their miraculous deliverance from Pharaoh, and their eventual possession of the promised land served as inspiration, comfort, and hope. Christianity alone, adulterated, otherworldly, and disengaged from its most authentic implications—as it was usually presented to the slaves—could not have provided the spiritual, emotional, and communal resources necessary for the kind of resistance they expressed. The volatile ingredients of the African religious past were essential enrichments as was, most important of all, the human yearning for freedom that found a channel for expression in the early Black Church.[52]

The Early Black Church

The processes by which Black churches achieved separation from their larger White counterparts and a measure of self-governance varied from church to church, city to city, and region to region. However, it is apparent that prior to 1800, no Black church, North or South, with one known exception, evolved without some form of White denominational recognition,

49. Ephesians 6:5
50. Wilmore, *Black Religion and Black Radicalism*, 46.
51. Ibid., 60.
52. Ibid., 50.

trusteeship of land title, and/or certification to the government by respected White men that the Blacks involved would cause the slave system no trouble.[53] With complications such as this, the "actual" independence of historic Black churches cannot be defined and dated with precision. Even with dependable records, any objective level of "true" Black independence is impossible to establish, due to inescapable White dominance and, what Mechal Sobel terms, the "sub-rosa autonomy."[54]

The gamut of Black Church independence runs from congregations heavily dominated by White sponsors, "to those who found subtle, creative ways to assert their underground independence and follow their own wills" as Black congregations.[55] While in most cases the separation was somewhat amicable, the inevitable separation by race came to a head with the organization of Black churches in the latter half of the eighteenth century. Externally, the clear basis for the separation may have appeared to be antipathy or prejudice, but internally it was clearly due to the differences in class, culture, and control. The class factor evolved as White denomination members began to ascend in social and economic status. Once such status was achieved, these same White members became uncomfortable with, and distanced themselves from, their fellow Black members. This sentiment was so prevalent in some instances that it became the impetus behind White members seeking the outright eviction of Black members, as in the case of St. George's Methodist Church in 1787.[56]

In similar fashion, the culture of worship became a point of divergence. What for Black members had served as cultural affirmation in the form of worship, eventually became embarrassment for fellow White members as they became "more affluent and socially respectable."[57] Yet, of greater significance was White reluctance and refusal to share organizational power and control. As Black members sought to actively participate as all rights and privileged members, specifically voting in denominational matters, White power structures began to revoke privileges and exclude membership. Mitchell writes:

> [T]he crucial issue of control at times rendered bitter even the otherwise heroic educational efforts of white denominations in the

53. Mitchell, *Black Church Beginnings*.
54. Sobel, *Trabelin' On*, 205.
55. Mitchell, *Black Church Beginnings*, 48.
56. Ibid., 52.
57. Ibid.

South after the Civil War. Even in the post-World War II era, the greatest challenge facing ethnically or racially "transitional" congregations has been, and still is, how to settle the issues of culture and control. In other words, the ones who provide the financial resources tend to insist on control, but those who provide the participants want equality of vote, regardless of how much they can or cannot give.[58]

Black Church Missional Ecclesiology

Integration of Mission, Liberation, & Participation

An essential clarifying point when discussing mission from the Black Church perspective must be that Black Church formation was not motivated by dissension over doctrinal conceptualizations. Black churches were formed as intentional religious communities attempting to provide worship environments free from racist practices. Borrowing from Emily Dickinson, William Lindsey argues,

> prophetic speech talks about what those in power talk about but it does so slant and circuitously, opening up the controlled world of the discourse community to an imagination entirely different from the one mandated from on high, and yet so compellingly believable that we wonder why no one has pointed this out before.[59]

The missional ecclesiology of the Black Church draws from this essential characteristic. As previously mentioned, African slaves appropriated metaphoric images derived from biblical texts in order to contemplate their social conditions and contexts. From an ecclesial perspective, these images were appropriated in order to interpret the Church's mission and ministry in the world, a stark contrast to the typical, apologetic categories related to the creedal formulas used to evaluate the theological and institutional character of the Church.[60]

---

58. Ibid., 53.

59. Lindsey, "Telling it Slant," 88–103.

60. In studying the ecclesiology of Black churches, the temptation to begin with creedal concepts exists, particularly the Nicene Creed—the one, holy, catholic, and apostolic church. These dimensions are useful in formulating a universal, and more general, theological understanding of the Church. While relevant, they do not comprise the distinctive qualities of Black ecclesiology.

THE FUTURE HORIZON FOR A PROPHETIC TRADITION

On this point, James Cone insightfully argues that the reduction of ecclesiology to only such human criteria confers an undesirable legitimacy to the historically racist practices of White Christian churches. Instead, some transcendent understanding of mission is critical to the integrity of the Black Church. While the Nicene Creed criteria traditionally outlines the transcendent character and authority of the Church, the Church, for Black-religious life, ultimately represents a people who have been called together and sent out by God's self-revelation in the liberating gospel message of Jesus Christ and who share in the activity of the Holy Spirit in the liberation of humanity.[61]

Liberation plays a pivotal role in the ecclesiology of the Black Church and thereby remains an undisputed criterion in its mission. While a transcendent understanding of the Black Church, and its functions, provides the essential qualification for an existential hermeneutic in ecclesiology, the liberation criterion sustains the viability of any existential approach. Since the inception of Black churches occurred in conjunction with abusive social practices and theological interpretations, such an existential hermeneutic is not merely possible but necessary. An existential hermeneutic in ecclesiology suggests that knowledge is derived from social context, which in turn contributes to individual and communal horizons of—for the sake of this argument, *religious*—meaning.[62] Though filled with pain, the horizon of Black experience must be engaged and addressed because underneath the pain of historical trauma lies creative and sustaining power—spiritual, intellectual and emotional. It then follows that a self-conscious Black missional ecclesiology emanates from the painful Black experience of oppression, which in turn not only accents liberation, but active participation in its pursuit as well.

Conclusion

I have attempted to outline the missional ecclesiological conversation as it relates to the context and calling of the Black Church. This is significant because it distinguishes the social conditions surrounding the Black Church

---

61. Cone, *Black Theology and Black Power*, 63–65.

62. The use of the word "horizons" means that one learns to look beyond what is close at hand, not in order to look away from it, but in order to see what is close at hand in a better way, that is, within a larger whole and thereby in truer proportion and perspective. See Gadamer, *Truth and Method*, 304.

and establishes the cultural realities in which its missionary impetus originated. This experience and reality work to produce the premise and practice of the Black Church that came to exemplify its communal nature. We will now turn to the theological framework that sharpens these reflections and begins to discern how the Black experience has necessitated a public faith characterized by the Black Church.

Chapter Two

Interpretative Dilemma

Introduction

As DISCUSSED IN THE previous chapter, the social conditions that surrounded the Black Church, namely slavery, contributed to its cultural comprehension, contextualization, and appropriation of scripture. This means that those who called themselves the Black Church, identified themselves as such due to the oppressive history of slavery in America. Christian theological ethicist H. Richard Niebuhr makes the point that when specific ideals are brought into any institution there is a loss of the original ideals that were already established.[1] Sociologically, Black Christian identity was established as a refuge for those looking and needing to withstand societal forces either working against them, not working in their interest, or both. In this chapter, I illuminate the Black Church's response to the White churches' accommodation to an American way of life—a way of life that prioritized and preferred social practices over and above the religious loyalties that it appeared to claim.

The Legacy of the Black Church

Public faith[2] has played a significant role in many of America's most important movements, including, for instance, this country's movement for independence from Great Britain in the 1770s, where "at every stage in

---

1. Niebuhr, *The Social Sources of Denominationalism*.

2. Public faith being defined as the non-privatized warranted religious activity, i.e. a privatized faith being the displacement of one's religious beliefs to the subjective sphere of self, rendering it irrelevant to the institutional functioning of society.

that momentous era, American Christians were present, involved, and even in the forefront of promoting an independent United States of America."[3] While the Black experience does not originate with the establishment of a country, it is associated with disenfranchisement within a country—namely, the Black experience in America, "which was and is a very singular illustration of the complexities of the human predicament, and of the spiritual resources available to the black church's mission to overcome."[4] So, to begin exploring the legacy of the Black Church, one must first understand that America began with slavery as a normal, acceptable, practical reality. According to Michael Battle, to be Black was

> to be a member of a cultural and linguistic nation, defined, in part, by its West African cultural heritage, by its forcible removal from Africa, by its estrangement from the cultures of both its mainly white context and its own past, by the ultimately unintelligible modern European concept of "race", and by shared experiences in slavery and segregation.[5]

These factors foundationally shaped the Black Church in that they fostered among people a deep faith in a supreme God who sympathized with the plight and problems of His people, specifically, the existential crisis of slavery. So, the White interpretation of Christianity, which effectively divested slaves of any concern about freedom, was transformed into what is today the Black Church.[6] In this regard, the Black Church lived in a different *Imago Dei* through its integration of individual and community, connecting spirituality and social witness with welcoming the stranger, thereby displaying a real inter-relationality that did not separate human identity from the divine presence of God. On a communal level, the relationship between the ongoing historical narrative and spiritual behavior defines the Black Church, a consequence, argues Black Church scholar Michael Battle, "of encountering a community with a constant, alternative narrative that leads to a radical interpretation of the old narrative, or the holistic creation of a new one."[7] In other words, the foundations of the Black Church developed out of the necessity to redefine Black identity, using Christianity

---

3. Knoll, *One Nation Under God?* 35.
4. Billingsley, *Mighty Like a River*, xx.
5. Battle, *The Black Church in America*, 51–52.
6. Ibid., 55.
7. Ibid., 27.

not so much as it was delivered to them by racist white churches, but as its truth was authenticated to them in the experience of suffering and struggle, to reinforce an enculturated religious orientation and to produce an indigenous faith that emphasized dignity, freedom, and human welfare.[8]

The result was an evolution of the Black Church from its beginnings as a source of solace and solidarity for the enslaved, to its central position in the struggle for liberation, becoming a beacon of courage with a will for the marginalized within society to resist further oppression and inequity.

From the 1800s, since the time of David Walker, Denmark Vesey, and Nat Turner, a radical biblical appropriation began to occur, the central thrust of which, according to Black Church history professor Charles Hamilton, "was to redefine the meaning and role of the church and religion in the lives of black people."[9] This hermeneutical change provided the contextual challenge to develop a theology that was not only Christian, but also relevant for the social and political needs of this particular people. This change shifted the discourse of the conversation from the individualistic tone embellished by larger society, to a communal tune embodied by the Black Church.

Saturated with biblical reference and prophecy, David Walker's *Appeal to the Coloured Citizens of the World*, published in 1829, stands as an iconic religious document of the Protestant era, drawing favorable comparisons to Martin Luther's *"Open Letter to the Christian Nobility of the German Nation"* from notable Black scholars and theologians.[10] Walker took liberative aim at many social theories and practices of the time, including Thomas Jefferson's well-known theory of Black inferiority, slavery in the United States, and the scheme of Black colonization proffered as a solution to the race problem since the time of the Revolutionary War.[11] Ultimately, Walker's Appeal called for rebellion—urging Blacks to educate themselves, remove the shackles of slavery, "and fight in self-defense for freedom and dignity in the name of the Lord of hosts."[12] According to noted liberation theology scholar Gayraud S. Wilmore, through the excoriation and condemnation,

> an ultimately hopeful spirit breathes through [his] writing as he calls upon white Christians to count the cost of racial peace and

---

8. Wilmore, *Black Religion and Black Radicalism*, 25.
9. Hamilton, *The Black Preacher in America*, 140.
10. Wilmore, *Black Religion and Black Radicalism*, 62.
11. Aptheker, *One Continual Cry, David Walker's Appeal*.
12. Ibid.

to humble themselves before God in order that friendship and brotherhood can bless the land that must otherwise be soaked with blood.[13]

The revolutionary pursuit of freedom, equity, and equality instilled in many the will to vanquish themselves from oppressive conditions. The indomitable will became the spark that ignited a radical interpretation of Christianity. After purchasing his freedom in 1800 and settling in Charleston, South Carolina, Denmark Vesey, the "Methodist Conspirator," led a slave insurrection. With an absorbing interest in Black religion, Vesey became "engrossed in the study of the Scriptures and brought to his investigations some interpretations that were decidedly unorthodox and possibly African or West Indian in origin."[14] According to Wilmore, church meetings provided the opportunity for indoctrination into this unorthodox interpretation and preparation for revolt, as Vesey was

> a member of the Hampstead church, one of several black congregations that broke away from the white denomination that year. The class system of the independent African Methodist Association of Charleston was used as a recruitment and indoctrination vehicle as well as a communication network for revolt. All the leaders were members of the new independent black church.[15]

After the insurrection plot was revealed by a house servant, Vesey and his followers were either executed, transported out of South Carolina, banished from the United States, or severely beaten and discharged. The failed conspiracy, however, was neither viewed as in vain, nor did it dampen the ardor for liberation. In fact, the

> dismal failure and the terrible consequences were the price that had to be paid by blacks to shake the consciences of Americans. Black Christians continued to believe that God was aligned with them against the iniquitous system of slavery.[16]

In 1831, while a slave in Southampton County, Virginia, Nat Turner, the Baptist prophet of rebellion, discovered an important fact that White Christians had successfully concealed from slaves for more than two-hundred years—that contained within the biblical narrative was a demand

---

13. Wilmore, *Black Religion and Black Radicalism*, 66.
14. Stuckey, *The Ideological Origins of Black Nationalism*, 32–38.
15. Wilmore, *Black Religion and Black Radicalism*, 83–84.
16. Ibid., 87.

The Future Horizon for a Prophetic Tradition

of justice, as well as a liberationist understanding of the message of Jesus Christ, which set believers free from every dehumanizing principality and oppressive power.[17] Believing that he had been given a true knowledge of the faith, Turner began to think of himself as a minister of the gospel and began to spread his message throughout the area.[18] Convinced that God had given him a great work to perform, and insisting that the war be waged "upon a Christian basis,"[19] Turner led the bloodiest insurrection in American history. Causing one Black scholar to assert,

> Nat Turner's appropriation of another kind of Lord, his recognition of the meaning of Jesus . . . adumbrated the black theology which developed among black preachers from Henry Highland Garnet to Martin Luther, King Jr.—Jesus as the protagonist of radical social change.[20]

Two fundamental purposes animated the theological enterprise of the Black Church: first, the Black Church presented itself, implicitly or explicitly, as a specific vehicle for black liberation;[21] and second, it regarded its engagement as a Christian mandate. For the Black Church, the struggle for liberation from any and every kind of oppression was consistent with the gospel, and every theological statement must parallel, and perpetuate, the goals of liberation. Liberation, therefore, must engage multiple forms of bondage—social, cultural, political, economic—and the Black Church must be a spiritually-defined, determined, and dutiful advocate. Even before the founding of Black religious institutions, Black public protest was cast in explicitly religious terms,[22] so it follows that the Black Church would become a social, economic, and political vehicle that provided for slaves and freed persons of color what no other institution was willing, or capable, of doing. Thus, spiritual uplift permeated every aspect of Black communal life that

> brought the comfort and the security of God's love and redemption into the hopelessness of abject dereliction. The black response—the prayer and the preaching, the singing, the moaning,

---

17. Johnson, *The Nat Turner Insurrection*.
18. Ibid.
19. Williams, *A History of the Negro Race in America, 1619–1883*, 88–90.
20. Wilmore, *Black Religion and Black Radicalism*, 90.
21. Black liberation being defined as transforming the black condition from oppression to authentic humanity.
22. As early as 1774, Africans in Massachusetts petitioned for release from their condition as "slaves for Life in a Christian land." Savage, *Your Spirits Walk Among Us*.

the shouting (or as Du Bois put it, "the frenzy")—kept human spirit alive and the presence of God an assured consolation.[23]

Two specific narratives functioned as *modi operandi* for the Black Church—the Exodus story and Jesus' suffering on the cross—both of which provoke an invitation to discover new meanings of human identity and community. The Exodus story resonated with Blacks as they likened themselves to the children of Israel—"involuntary adhesions to a host society in which their creative participation was severely limited by law, by tradition, and by caprice."[24] An identity as God's new chosen people created a community of faith[25] in the face of White scholars' adamant refusal to acknowledge Egypt's historical significance and geographical connection to people of color. To combat the debilitating implications that the White scholars' refusal had on Black identity, Black Christian liberation encouraged "the idea that black people were not 'cursed of God,' nor condemned by God to be 'hewers of wood and drawers of water' for the white people who called themselves 'masters.'"[26]

In this manner, the appropriation of the Almighty, transformed Black corporate identity from an imposed social condition to a cognitive understanding of belonging, enabling a transcendent cohesion of African American and faith identity as a people of God.[27] The Old Testament notion of God as liberator anchored the experience of suffering and struggle in an evolving truth. It reinforced an enculturated religious orientation and produced an indigenous faith that emphasized dignity, freedom, and human welfare. So, Black people began to identify themselves not as the cursed descendants of Ham,[28] but as the children of enslaved and liberated Israel, with America, once thought by the Puritans to be the Promised Land, posited as Egypt—thus equating God with the God of the suffering and oppressed.

In the heart, mind, and spirit of Black folk, the cruciform Jesus provoked an inspired pursuit to discover new meanings of human identity and community. Within the cross is a declaration of self-withdrawing and self-giving love, which manifests a power "to commit oneself to reorganize

23. Billingsley, *Mighty Like A River*, xxiii.
24. Ibid., xx.
25. Raboteau, *Slave Religion*, 311.
26. Billingsley, *Mighty Like A River*, xxiii.
27. Andrews, *Practical Theology for Black Churches*, 43.
28. A theory suggested and supported by many White slaveowners, as well as the group called "American school of anthropology." Genovese, *Roll, Jordan, Roll*.

identity in the service of empowering others."[29] To be identified with Christ, His disciples are called to deny themselves, take up their cross, and follow Him.[30] Thus, authentic "Christian identity and theology have a cruciform shape, but the meaning and significance of the cross must be reinterpreted in relation to particular contexts."[31] So, the Black Church became, as C. Eric Lincoln characterized, "a precipitate of its *own* culture, developed from, and in response to, its own experience."[32] This became, according to Battle, "the incredible achievement of the Black Church: to make seamless human incorporation into the pursuit of God's peace and justice demonstrated in the life, death, and resurrection of Jesus."[33] Furthermore, to counter the contrasting rhetoric of Church versus state, the Black Church helped to crystallize that all civic responsibilities are an obligation of Christian service as it constructed a new politic of self, community, and society based on its reinterpretation and reapplication of Scripture. As Karl Barth offers, John 3:16 does not say, "For God so loved the *Christians* . . . " but "For God so loved the *world* . . . "[34]

On this continuum of reinterpretation and reapplication, the Black Church began to recognize the need for a completely new "starting point" in theology, insisting that this "starting point" be defined by people at the bottom as opposed to those at the top of the socioeconomic ladder.[35] It is of paramount importance to convey that the Black Church challenged coercive ideologies that constructed a framework within which the dominant culture deprived others of their identity. Yet, because the spirituality of the Black Church was interpersonal and communal, it sought the new creation of a civic community that could sustain basic opportunities for, and relationships among, all people—oppressor and oppressed, Black and White, rich and poor.[36]

---

29. Battle, *The Black Church in America*, 31.
30. See Matthew 16:24, Mark 8:34, Luke 9:23
31. Battle, *The Black Church in America*, 31.
32. Billingsley, *Mighty Like A River*, xxi.
33. Battle, *The Black Church in America*, 44.
34. Karl Barth, *Church Dogmatics*, 559.
35. Battle, *The Black Church in America*, 99.
36. Lovin, "Civil Rights, Civil Society, and Christian Realism."

The Civil Rights Movement

Among other things, effective movements highlight issues and values in a manner that marries reality with expectation in the public sphere. Deeply troubled by White Christianity's convenient overlooking of racism, the civil rights movement, through the Black Church, "came together as a united witness of communal spirituality."[37] Due to the interpersonal and communal spirituality of the Black Church, the active participation and pursuit of civil rights was an existential response derived from the purpose and location of the Black Church. Many of the civil rights movement's leaders came from the Black Church, and they articulated the theological basis for the social transformation the movement was advocating. Chief among these leaders was Martin Luther King, Jr. Historian J. Deotis Roberts reminds that,

> Without the black church tradition, there would not have been a Martin Luther King Jr. as we know him. Without the religious experience that steeled black sufferers against hardships and inflamed their consciences against injustices, King would not have emerged as it were from the womb of the black church.[38]

In articulating the struggle for civil rights, King defined the biblical term *"agape"* as love in action that seeks to preserve and create community. He highlighted four aspects of agape: insistence on community even when others seek to break it, willingness to sacrifice in the interest of mutuality, willingness to go to any length to restore community, and going the second, third, even fourth mile if necessary. Action, therefore, took the form of organizing, mobilizing, marching and protesting, so that one's creed matched one's deeds.[39] King wrote:

> One of the great tragedies of life is that men seldom bridge the gulf between practice and profession, between doing and saying. A persistent schizophrenia leaves so many of us tragically divided against ourselves. On the one hand, we proudly profess certain sublime and noble principles, but on the other hand, we sadly practice the very antithesis of those principles. How often are our lives characterized by a high blood pressure of creeds and an anemia of deeds![40]

---

37. Battle, *The Black Church in America*, 127.
38. Roberts, *Black Religion, Black Theology*, 58.
39. King Jr., *Stride Toward Freedom the Montgomery Story*, 105.
40. King Jr., *Strength to Love*, 40.

King's biblical precedent for this point is the New Testament Epistle of James, which reads:

> You do well if you really fulfill the royal law according to the scripture, "You shall love your neighbor as yourself." But if you show partiality, you commit sin, and are convicted by the law as transgressors . . . What good is it, my brothers and sisters, if you say you have faith but do not have works? Can faith save you? If a brother or sister is naked and lacks daily food, and one of you says to them, "Go in peace; keep warm and eat your fill," and yet you do not supply their bodily needs, what is the good of that? So faith by itself, if it has no works, is dead.[41]

James suggests that genuine faith, as personally held, is to be publicly practiced, naturally producing good works. In fact, faith and works are complementary. When an individual truly believes in a cause, that belief will change the way the person lives. As a result, creeds become deeds. True faith and righteous actions go hand-in-hand as they comprise the work of God's servants—the calling of the Holy Spirit brings an individual to faith, while the conviction of the Holy Spirit brings the individual to faithfulness. Privately held, "actions" embody a personal character that seeks to comprehend God's will in a particular situation through rigorous effort to clarify unconditional moral duties. Publicly practiced, "actions" embody a political character, which comes to understand God by prudently acting together with others in public struggle to redress some social or economic injustice.[42] The issue, therefore, for the Black Church at the time of the civil rights movement was not whether one's private faith should come to public expression—the two could not be separated—but rather, to what *extent* one's public expression should be informed by one's personal faith.

Institutionally, the Black Church helped define the terms in which American democracy and freedom would be discussed as it demonstrated to the rest of American religious communities how faith could be a driving force for serving the common good. The result of this process was twofold: first, the goal to fully participate in American society; and second, the collaborative effort of citizens that extended beyond ethnic, class, and racial differences.[43] The Black Church was committed to protecting the rights of all people living into God's image, eschatologically portraying the Kingdom

---

41. James 2:8–9, 14–17 NRSV
42. Kelsey, *To Understand God Truly*, 47.
43. Nelsen and Nelsen, *Black Church in the Sixties*.

of God as a time and place that invites persons to be of one accord—acknowledging, accepting, and valuing difference in the common society. It asserted that God's interest was not merely in the freedom of black, brown and yellow, but rather, as King testified, "in the freedom of the whole human race and in the creation of a society where all men [sic] can live together as brothers, where every man will respect the dignity and the worth of human personality."[44] An eschatological vision of hope became a primary emphasis in the Black Church that sustained and nurtured the practical quest for liberation. For the Black Church, "other-worldly" and "this-worldly" are not separate. What initially appears to be a divergence, realistically amounts to a convergence, as heavenly mandates lead to earthly practices, which, in turn, brings about present action and ways of being.[45]

Exploring the dichotomy between the present and future as it relates to the meaning of biblical eschatology, Hans Küng asks, "What does the reign of God, which is already irrupting into the present, mean for the concrete existence of [humankind], what meaning does it give to [human] life here and now?"[46] For the civil rights movement, influenced by the prophetic impulse of the Black Church, eschatology became inextricably linked both to immediate survival and a vibrant expectancy that preserved the hope necessary for living in the present age.[47]

For King and the civil rights movement, the concept of community included a prophetic vision of an eschatological society in which those in conflict may one day live without oppression.[48] To make the connection between Jesus and social justice, King argued,

> The gospel at its best deals with the whole man, not only with his soul but also with his body, not only his spiritual well-being but also his material well-being. A religion that professes concern for the souls of men and is not equally concerned about the slums that damn them, the economic conditions that strangle them, and the social conditions that cripple them, is a spiritually moribund religion.[49]

This connection between moral obligation and social location was deeply rooted in the prophetic tradition. How then does this connection be

44. Washington, *A Testament of Hope.*
45. Cummings, "The Slave Narratives as a Source of Black Theological Discourse."
46. Küng, *The Church,* 61.
47. Andrews, *Practical Theology for Black Churches,* 48; also Küng, *The Church,* 66.
48. Battle, *The Black Church in America,* 133.
49. King Jr., *Strength to Love,* 149.

recontextualized to confront the contemporary conditions challenging the Black community?

The Importance of Pastoral Leadership

Arguably, the Black preacher is the most important and influential figure in Black culture. Within the church, the preacher is expected to provide spiritual guidance, organizational leadership, and congregational direction. The expectation is that s/he be a great orator, study the bible thoroughly, and deliver inspiring sermons. The scope of the Black preacher's responsibilities range from blessing newborn children, to planning and presiding over funeral services—all while simultaneously being available to congregants at any given time. Due to this high visibility and influence in, and on, the community, the Black preacher is often called upon to provide leadership outside of the church.

Just as Martin Luther, John Wesley, and others had no desire to form new churches, so the Black preacher would have chosen otherwise had viable options been available. Since the formation of Black churches was not motivated by dissension over doctrinal conceptualizations, but formed as intentional religious communities attempting to provide worship environments free from racist practices, the Black preacher became the preeminent, pulpit paradigm—able to influence, inform, incite, and inspire. In other words, Black preachers "have always been in a state of readiness, at least theoretically, to move from a so-called conservative mode into quite a different style, depending on the circumstances."[50] From slave quarters to contemporary contexts, the purpose and meaning of the Black preacher have not greatly changed in the traditional churches, sects, and cults of the Black community. Whether channeling contempt or rousing rebellion, the Black preacher sounds the trumpet to reach the masses, release power, and reaffirm purpose.

During slavery, the Black preacher's creative rendition of the eschatological passages of the Old and New Testaments became a means to draw people from the edge of hopelessness, to the horizon of possibility. The preacher continued, therefore, to propagate the pragmatic implications of the biblical message—"that the day would surely come when the truth of the gospel of liberation would be manifest."[51] More than 130 years after the hanging of Nat Turner, Black clergy in many major denominations began

50. Paris, *The Social Teaching of the Black Churches*, 52.
51. Wilmore, *Black Religion and Black Radicalism*, 75.

to reassess the relationship of the Christian church to the Black community. Black caucuses developed in Catholic, Presbyterian, and Episcopal churches with the central purpose being to redefine the meaning and role of the church and religion in the lives of Black people.[52] For the first time in the history of Black religious thought, according to Battle, Black clergy began to recognize the need for a completely new "starting point" in theology. They insisted that this starting point must be defined by those in the margins of society, as opposed to those in the middle. So, the Black preacher "began to reread the Bible through the eyes of their slave grandparents and started to speak of God's solidarity with the oppressed of the earth."[53]

From their meeting with General William T. Sherman and Secretary of War Edwin Stanton to discuss the implementation of the Emancipation Proclamation, through the formative phases of the civil rights movement, up to rallying behind Barack Obama's presidential election, Black clergy have

> sought not to access a set of opportunities already in existence, but the creation of a new civic community that could sustain basic opportunities for and relationships among people historically oppressed in American society and around the world.[54]

Indeed, from the time of emancipation, Black clergy have immersed themselves in electoral politics to effect change and meet the social needs of their community. When newly freed Black men had their first opportunities for open political engagement, religious institutions provided the organizational infrastructure for mass political mobilization. So it just made sense that Black clerics—the most educated, revered, and recognizable figures in the Black community—would seek public office. Black clerics were particularly prominent in Reconstruction politics. One historian estimates that over 100 Black ministers, from African Methodist Episcopal to Primitive Baptist, were elected to legislative seats during Reconstruction, noting that ministers used their churches as a political launching point.[55]

Individualism and the drive for personal wealth accumulation symbolize a modern new threat to the integrity of today's Black preacher. The mantra of prosperity, rather than the biblical mission of love, service, and justice, more accurately describes the chief aim of many Black Church

---

52. Hamilton, *The Black Preacher in America*, 140.
53. Battle, *The Black Church in America*, 99.
54. Lovin, "Civil Rights, Civil Society, and Christian Realism."
55. Foner, *Reconstruction*, 93.

leaders. Having earned a noble place in the complicated history of American democracy and Christianity, the Black preacher demonstrated to the rest of American communities that faith could function as a force for serving the common good. The Black preacher helped to define the terms in which American democracy and freedom would be discussed.[56] The single greatest threat to the historical legacy and core values of contemporary Black Church leadership is their reluctance to walk in the prophetic tradition of critiquing and challenging the society in which they live. This is symptomatic of a larger crisis of purpose that has placed the Black preacher in a posture of pragmatic accommodationism, avoiding extremely conservative or liberal political views, and thus cooperating and compromising with the social, political, and corporate status quo.[57] Conforming to society is not a new challenge, but with two conditions firmly in place—Christianity as a dominant religion, and a nation that rewards and permits extraordinary disparities of wealth and power—the new face of an old problem constitutes the crux of the issues facing the Black preacher: assimilation sanctifies personal greed, obsessive materialism, and unchecked narcissism. This leads to a more thorough and comprehensive distortion of the gospel and self-centered, individualistic leadership that dares not critique unjust social systems and practices.

Asserting a crisis in Black leadership, Cornel West suggests that today's leaders lack two qualities that were present among the past leaders of the civil rights era: anger and humility. The irony is that many of today's Black preachers strategically present themselves as relevant, powerful, and accepted individuals while doing nothing to risk their access to important people or revenue streams in order to achieve "higher ground" goals in the area of social justice.[58] Black preacher activity should become more than the usual "gossip topic" in the village[59] and instead become a cause for community action that identifies, cultivates, and constructively critiques authentic leaders. In order to demand a new level of accountability among Black Church leadership, a new culture of village responsibility will be necessary. The community needs to "call out," or openly challenge, their leaders and request a declaration of their vision for serving and transforming the

---

56. Franklin, *Crisis in the Village*, 106.

57. Franklin, *Another Day's Journey*, 44.

58. Cornel West, *Race Matters*, 51–70.

59. For example, the extra-marital affair and financial misappropriation of Reverend Henry Lyons, former President of the National Baptist Convention.

community.⁶⁰ The renewal of the Black preacher depends on a reckoning with the significant social, political, and economic changes that have occurred in Black communities since the Civil Rights Movement.

Currently, despite struggles of the past, the issue of race continues to plague American society—a fact that is supported by the huge racial disparities in education, health, and income-level among others. This lack of recognition regarding the significant role played by race in American policies and practices serves to perpetuate social inequities. According to social historian Manning Marble,

> Race is a dynamic, changing social relationship grounded in structural inequality. As the human composition of American society's social order has shifted, the lived reality of structural racism has also changed in everyday existence. What has remained constant, unfortunately, is that "blackness," no matter how it is constituted in ethnic terms, has continued to be stigmatized and relegated to the periphery of power and opportunity.⁶¹

The election of the United States' first Black president is clearly the product of a social trajectory that denies race or racism. Barack Obama's successful presidential campaign and the general social climate in which we live furthers the myth of meritocracy that many Americans accept about what it means to be citizens in this country. The myth centers on equality and opportunity for everyone who "works hard," but for most Blacks, the myth is quickly destroyed by the realities of daily life.

In addition to the political realities, there is an economic dimension as well. In his work, *Being in the Black, Living In The Red: Race, Wealth, and Social Policy* in America, Dalton Conley critically analyzes the relationship between race and wealth accumulation. The current system of free market capitalism, through which, allegedly, anyone who works hard can succeed, operates on several principles that are crippling to many Blacks. According to Conley, savings and investments are important for growing the American economy, but Blacks have been under-and unpaid labor for an extended period of time, with only the last fifty years offering opportunities to amass wealth.⁶² Therefore, there has been no significant accumulation of wealth in Black communities, definitively disproportionate to White communities, "since wealth accumulation depends heavily on intergenerational support

---

60. Franklin, *Crisis in the Village*, 133.
61. Marable, *Living Black History*, 208.
62. Conley, *Being Black, Living in the Red*.

such as gifts, informal loans, and inheritances."[63] With experience being a key element to increasing productivity under free market ideologies, the fact that Blacks have historically been shut out of many professional areas has meant that Blacks have not obtained the long-term experience considered necessary for professional advancement.

In order for a person to adapt to changing work environments, education is vital. Economist Marcellus Andrews believes,

> A highly educated work force that has extensive experience with rapidly changing technologies, and that can pass on knowledge of how to succeed in academic competition to its children, will be able to improve its ability to work over time, quite apart from any investments in new types of machines and production methods.[64]

But, he continues, Blacks have had unequal access to education as part of the considerable legacy of historic underinvestment in the human capital of Blacks.[65] This confluence of economic factors has created market-driven segregation as the middle-class uses its higher income to create economic and social distance from lower-classes, resulting in what Andrews concludes is nothing more than free-market racism.[66]

These ideas are supported by a variety of statistical data. In 1865, at the time of the Emancipation Proclamation, Blacks owned 0.5% of the total worth of the United States—not surprising seeing that most Blacks had been slaves up to that point. However, by 1990, a full 135 years after the abolition of slavery, Blacks owned a meager 1% of total wealth.[67] "In other words," according to Conley, "almost no progress had been made in terms of property ownership. African Americans may have won 'title' to their own bodies and to their labor, but they have gained ownership over little else.[68] Statistics augment Conley's point: Black unemployment rate is 14.8% (compared to 8.5% for Whites), less than half of Black families own a home (47.4%) compared to 75% of White families, Blacks are three times as likely, as compared to Whites, to live below the poverty line, 19.1% of Blacks are without healthcare insurance (10.8% for Whites), and the median Black household earning is $34,218 (compared to $55,530 for White

63. Ibid., 6.
64. Andrews, *The Political Economy of Hope and Fear*, 121.
65. Ibid., 122.
66. Ibid., 148.
67. Anderson, *Black Labor, White Wealth*.
68. Conley, *Being Black, Living in the Red*, 25.

households).⁶⁹ Although as a group Blacks have made progress in a number of socioeconomic areas, the base from which they began was dismally low. For instance, in 1964, only 9.4% of Blacks held professional or managerial positions, compared to 24.7% of Whites.⁷⁰ Statistics aside, the conditions and issues plaguing urban areas throughout this country—Flint, Michigan water controversy, lack of affordable housing, high incarceration rates of Black men between the ages of 20 and 35—continue to evidence that substantial racial inequities remain in the United States.

Another challenge in preparing responsive Black pastoral leaders is to address what Sharon Daloz Parks refers to as five key hungers that conspire to create a growing crisis in leadership: personal agency, authority, ability to deal with complexity, adaptive response, and the creation of a new moral moment.⁷¹ If the Black preacher is ineffective or inept, it may be due to a lack of proficiency in navigating among, and negotiating with, the public institutions and systems within the social environment. Franklin argues that the Black preacher must become a public theologian, committed to not only presenting spiritual understandings, but also ethical principles and values for public scrutiny, discussion, and possible acceptance. In contrast to sectarian theologians who understand that they are speaking for and to the community of believers, public theologians understand themselves as "ambassadors for Christ," standing between worlds, representing the distinctive vision and virtues of Christianity to a secular culture.⁷²

An awful legacy of slavery preserved by many African ancestors is the mistrust of others manifested in competition with one another. During slavery, the competition was to earn the good will of the master. Malcolm X, more than any other contemporary leader, sought to demolish this sentiment and instill more cooperative and trusting working relationships throughout the Black community and abroad. In order to transform communities, the Black preacher must bring to a close the current culture of inefficiency, duplication, and "silo survival." This is a call for leaders who are collaborative and cooperative thinkers committed to renewing communal relationships within civil society. The preceding eras have taught that if any institutional and systemic impact is to be made, it will come via broad and

---

69. National Urban League, *Jobs 2010 The State of Black America: Responding to the Crisis*.

70. Hochschild, *Facing Up to the American Dream*, 55.

71. Parks, *Leadership Can Be Taught*.

72. Franklin, *Another Day's Journey*, 122.

nonpartisan coalitions, whose sole purpose is effecting change. The power and influence of the preacher remains exceedingly important. Whether viewed as cultural reformists or thoroughgoing radicals, the vocal presence of Black leadership challenges the sacred grounding of society itself.[73] This has been the implicit danger in all moral reform efforts, particularly those activities of the historic Black preacher, which take aim at institutional, systemic and structural change. We should remember that the calling of the Black preacher emerged out of slavery and the Black Church was born out of the nation's race problem. With many social, economic, and political problems still intact, especially in the Black community, the need for the Black Church and Black preacher/prophet continues.

Liberation and Prophetic Engagement

Liberation and prophetic engagement continue to be major concerns for the Black Church and community. Indeed, several recent discussions and publications among Black preachers and scholars have focused on the legacy and future of a social gospel.[74] Before proceeding with this section, I must highlight a few noteworthy considerations. First, the term Black is used in definitive conjunction with, not contradiction of, Negro, Colored, Afro-, and African-American. Throughout history, each of these has been used progressively and interchangeably to refer to persons of color who do not identify with Asian, Hispanic, or Native ethnicities. Second, I recognize that congregants enter Black churches with a multitude of identities that shape their experiences. Thus, while my inquiry is focused on understanding commonalities across the Black Church, I acknowledge the importance of recognizing the diversity within this population with regard to gender, sexual orientation, social/class/generational status, and so forth.

According to the U.S. Religious Landscape Survey, conducted in 2007 by the Pew Research Center's Forum on Religion & Public Life, while the United States is generally considered a highly religious nation, Blacks are markedly more religious on a variety of measures than the United States population as a whole—including level of affiliation with a religion, attendance at religious services, frequency of prayer, and the significance of religion. Compared with other racial and ethnic groups, African-Americans are among the most likely

---

73. Paris, *The Social Teaching of the Black Churches*, 58.
74. Hopkins and Thomas, *Walk Together Children*.

to report a formal religious affiliation, with 87% of Blacks describing themselves as belonging to one religious group or another.

The Landscape Survey also finds that nearly eight-in-ten Blacks (79%) say religion is very important in their lives, compared with 56% among all United States adults. In fact, a large majority (72%) of Blacks who are unaffiliated with any particular faith say religion plays at least a somewhat important role in their lives; nearly half (45%) of unaffiliated Blacks say religion is very important in their lives, which is roughly three times the percentage of those who say this among the religiously unaffiliated population overall (16%). Additionally, several measures illustrate the distinctiveness of the Black community when it comes to religious practices and beliefs. More than half of Blacks (53%) report attending religious services at least once a week, more than three-in-four (76%) conduct prayer on a daily basis and nearly nine-in-ten (88%) indicate they are absolutely certain that God exists. On each of these measures, Blacks stand out as the most religiously committed racial or ethnic group in the nation. Even those Blacks who are unaffiliated with any religious group pray nearly as often as the overall population of mainline Protestants (48% of unaffiliated Blacks pray daily vs. 53% of all mainline Protestants). And unaffiliated Blacks are about as likely to believe in God with absolute certainty (70%) as are mainline Protestants (73%) and Catholics (72%) overall.

The Landscape Survey also shows that the link between religion and some social and political attitudes in the Black community is very similar to that seen among the population overall. For instance, just as in the general public, Blacks who are more religiously observant (as defined by frequency of worship service attendance and the importance of religion in their lives) are more likely to oppose abortion and homosexuality and more likely to report higher levels of conservative ideology. It is important to emphasize, however, that differences on political and social issues across religious groups within the Black community tend to be smaller than among the population overall. Compared with other groups, Blacks express a high degree of comfort with religion's role in politics. In fact, in a subsequent survey, Blacks tended to closely resemble White Evangelical Protestants on that score, with roughly six-in-ten among both groups saying that churches should express their views on social and political topics, and roughly half saying that there has been too little expression of faith and prayer by political leaders.[75]

---

75. Source: Survey conducted summer 2008 by Pew Research Center for the People

The Future Horizon for a Prophetic Tradition

Religion and Politics

While the current preaching trend is to promote success and prosperity, the historic role of the prophetic preacher in promoting a social gospel has been integral to the Black community.[76] Religion and politics in the United States have always significantly interacted. This is more so true for African-Americans, since the Black Church is central to African American social, economic, and political life. The connections between Black religion and civil institutions range from the role that Black churches played in sponsoring early and after-school programs to the disproportionately high numbers of Black clergy and churches involved in electoral politics. These latter habits carve an important caricature of much African American civic culture, which involves such matters as beliefs, attitudes, and general disposition toward political systems. The Black Church has long participated in and shaped an American civil religion that has endowed this nation with transcendent meaning and millennial destiny. This civic faith combines religion and nationalism, fusing American religious themes such as messianism, deliverance, and redemption with U.S. political ideals such as democracy, freedom, and equality. This country's faith, with its pool of symbols, myths, and rituals, seeks to merge the highly diverse, heterogeneous U.S. polity into a single national moral-spiritual community—a guiding principle of the Founding Fathers. The *concern* of religion and civil society differs from the *concept* of church and state. Failure to make this distinction results in confusion. Jefferson's concept of church and state has to do with institutions and practices, and neither must trespass the boundaries that define their legitimate sphere of influence. Jefferson's concept of separation is valid, but thorny in two particular areas: the first involves trying to navigate between establishment of religion and free exercise—prayer in public institutions is among the most contentious; the second arises when religious belief and practice conflict with secular law. The concern of religion and politics defines another set of issues. While church and state identifies the independence of institutions, religion and civil society outlines their interdependence in the lives of individuals. As Kenneth Cauthen notes, "citizens who belong to religious groups are also members of the secular society, and this dual-association generates complications."[77] While it may

---

& the Press and the Pew Forum.

76. Paris, *The Social Teaching of the Black Churches*.
77. Cauthen, *The Ethics of Belief*.

be true that religious beliefs have moral and social implications, and it may be appropriate for people of faith to express these through their activities as citizens within civic engagement, the fact that ethical convictions are rooted in religious faith should not disqualify them from the secular realm. However, they cannot be deemed secularly significant simply because they are thought by their exponents to be religiously mandated—they must be argued for in appropriate social and political terms that harmonize with national values. In both cases, according to Cauthen, "we should be prepared to deal with complexities, ambiguities, and overlapping realms in which practical discernment must find workable principles to guide us that are as compatible with fundamental Constitutional imperatives as human reason can devise."[78]

As Blacks coped with slavery and racial segregation, the religion that emerged out of that experience underwent various reforms, and what evolved was a civic tradition that cultivated identity and contributed to a heightened sense of citizenship. While Black religious traditions had different ideas concerning approaches to social conditions, during the civil rights era, most Black religious traditions arrived at a consensus concerning the need to be involved in addressing the oppressive, racist, and at the time, legal conditions affecting the Black community. As a mediating institution reflecting the interests of a marginalized population, Black Church beginnings privileged the holistic needs of its community—social, economic, and political; but like most institutions, the foundational warrants for the prioritizing of such activities became the basis for disagreement. Like most religious institutions, the Black Church primarily existed to meet the spiritual needs of its members, leading them to devote most of their resources to and for pastoral leadership. As the needs of the community began to change due to social conditions, the scope of the church's responsibility changed as well, giving rise to another civic tradition within the Black Church—prophetic engagement. With a more expansive view, the activist aspect within the Black Church, dating back to the Reconstruction era, began to surge.[79] That tradition of prophetic engagement and activism, especially when collaboratively approached, i.e., ministers aligning themselves to form urban political machines, gives basis for theological interpretation.

---

78. Ibid.
79. Billingsley, *Mighty Like a River*.

Institutional Interaction

Without a doubt, the Civil Rights and Black Power movements altered Black religious and secular institutions. It must be noted, however, that only a small number of Black ministers, churches, and civil institutions supported either. In recounting the success of the Montgomery Bus Boycott, Martin Luther King pointed to the difficulties of mobilizing support from Black ministers, noting their apathy stemmed from a sincere aversion to the earthy, temporal matters of social justice and economic improvement.[80] While these attitudes and actions were not rare, the success of the movements had long-term implications for the continued role of the Black Church. Since ministers were a visible part of the leadership cadre, and because of the emphasis on Christian values, the movements projected an image that the Black Church was the vanguard of social change. Since then, social relevancy has been a hallmark of the Black Church.

In general, prophetic engagement of Black churches has reflected the contextual opportunities and limitations operative within their current setting. For instance, with the enactment of the Civil Rights Act in 1964 and the Voting Rights Act in 1965, an altogether different context of Black Church involvement emerged as a result of unprecedented Black access to the processes and practices of American politics. Evidence of the historical settings and cultural shifts indicate the varied responses to social crises. As church-based community outreach programs evolved during the Reconstruction era, so did the prophetic engagement of the Black Church during the civil rights era of the 1950s and 1960s. As newly freed Black men were given the right to vote, Black churches provided the organizational resources to mobilize the new Black electorate—providing the "safe-space" for political gatherings, candidate connection, and volunteer recruitment.[81] Political platforms were regularly discussed from Black pulpits, as Black churches provided the only mechanism by which Black expression and connection could be unfiltered, uncompromised, and uninhibited. Political activism then began to take on a collaborative form as many Black churches worked in cooperation with civil rights groups such as the National Association for the Advancement of Colored People (NAACP) and the National Urban League (NUL). Aligning with these social organizations allowed political elites to employ churches as a direct vehicle for Black political participation.

80. King, Jr., *Stride Toward Freedom*.
81. Marable, *Race, Reform, and Rebellion*.

Political candidates made direct appeals before Black congregations and many Black ministers began to endorse candidates, promise support, and deliver votes—it was not unusual during a primary or general election campaign to see a number of White candidates on the agenda ready to present their claims for support during Sunday morning service, e.g., congressional candidate Keith Ellison and Senatorial candidate Al Franken frequenting several Twin Cities' area Black churches.

The pervasiveness of racism led Black Church leaders to conclude that systemic power was the most significant ingredient, and inhibitor, of their people's equality efforts. The sense of powerlessness compelled Black churches to take the lead in establishing an ethos to uplift the Black community—making the social gospel a foundational premise. The Black Church emphasized the perfectionist ideas that signaled an emerging holiness movement in American culture, and grounded those ideas in the conviction that the solution to social ills was the collective transformation of individuals, institutions, and systems.[82] The prophetic engagement of the Black Church, which came in its critique of current social, economic, and political practices, accounted for its most pronounced social relevance. In challenging America's deficiencies, namely the failures to deal justly and constructively with racial issues, the Black Church candidly called White society's attention to a vision of liberty with a more inclusive understanding of religion's participatory role within civil society.

Forced into the public arena by the very nature of the Black condition, the Black Church put aside concerns of church/state separation to engage in the work of making the Christian faith relevant to the struggle for social justice. As a result, Jefferson's concept of church/state separation became neither a principled nor a prudential statement, but rather a political reflection concerning the institutional arrangement of a system in which the Constitution was intended to guide—an arrangement that rendered the Black community voiceless. So, for the Black Church, this political reflection concerned the arrangement of institutions, not the obligation of individuals. Hence, the prophetic consciousness of the Black Church sought to attack contemporary circumstances at the core of America's moral purpose and social practices.

More than an organizational space, the Black Church acted as a theological interpreter of the Black experience in America. This understanding syncretized indigenous religious ideas and organic theologies into a specific Black theology of reconciliation—a theology rooted in specific

---

82. Crouch, Jr. and Gregory, *What We Love About the Black Church*.

understandings of bondage and oppression in Scripture.[83] In fact, Black theology is distinct because of its specific theodicy—the issue of reconciling God's justice in the presence of human suffering.[84] While not unique to Black theology, theodicy takes on a specific, racialized form in the Black religious experience. For Blacks, evil takes the identifiable form of White supremacy, enslavement, Jim Crow, or otherwise. Having to confront, if not resolve, this fundamental dilemma of God's love for Black people in the midst of oppression, segregation, and racialization is an implicit, as well as explicit, theological interpretation of reconciliation. While the earliest Black churches dissented relative to denominational identities, systems of polity, doctrinal standards, and modes of discipline, they assented regarding the fundamental need to challenge the status quo.[85] They had a common understanding of the Christian faith and its implications for addressing human need and inequality. In other words, there was an unanimity—beliefs, attitudes, values, and expectations—that bound them together despite the autonomy that distinguished one from the other. Thus, they were able to reconcile individual differences with a collective objective while dismantling divisive social practices with a divine vision for humanity.

Institutional Tension

The concept of "dual citizenship" has been used to define social condition and political complicatedness. It refers to individuals whose discriminatory and discretionary exclusion from inalienable rights take them on a quest for alternatives to the formal politics within their context amidst persons unsettled and uncertain in a modern setting with enduring loyalties to colonial approaches or imperial practices.[86] This duality can be drawn upon to talk about a type of tension felt within the Black Church as well as to shape how it can move forward. The Black Church has historically lived between acquiescence and agitation, secular standing and spiritual impulse, in an evolving effort to guide its participation in American civic life. A primary guide can be the literal interpretation of mission and destiny as "under God," albeit one civic scholar presents the dyad of "Nation under God" versus "Nation as Self-Transcendent" as one of the most fundamental

---

83. Mitchell, *Black Church Beginnings*.
84. Battle, *The Black Church in America*.
85. Crouch and Gregory, *What We Love About the Black Church*.
86. Andrews, *Practical Theology for Black Churches*.

divisions within American civil religion.[87] The "Under God" form positions the Judeo-Christian God as the origin of America's mission, which therefore remains always subject to divine authority and judgment. On the other hand, the "Nation as Self-Transcendent" form regards America's social-political system, and attributes such as democracy and free enterprise, as having intrinsic meaning with or without God. Believing that "all men were equal before God," and associating "moral evil with institutions of the external world," and holding that it was within the capacity of men to achieve salvation by unselfish deeds and unrelenting struggle against inward and outward evil, the Black Church's exercise of free will condemned domination, subjugation, and oppression and denounced those who sought them as usurpers of power that belonged only to God.[88]

A secondary guide can be a prophetic postulation which reconciles the critique of society with work toward effecting change. The position has as extremes dormancy and relevancy. Borrowing from Malcolm X,

> . . . when you've got some coffee that's too black, which means it's too strong, what do you do? You integrate it with cream . . . But if you pour too much cream in it, you won't even know you ever had coffee. It used to be hot, it becomes cool. It used to be strong, it becomes weak. It used to wake you up, now it puts you to sleep.[89]

This leaves little room for institutional compromise, relative to prophetic engagement, as far as the Black Church is concerned. When Black people collectively experienced racial oppression in similar ways, there was greater group solidarity. Racial integration has altered, in a fundamental way, the common ground that once served as a foundation for Black liberation struggle.[90] If the belief is that God has placed it in a unique position to speak truth to power, then action must be indicative of that premise and placement and the tension related to its location must be reconciled. That is to say, the church as refuge, grounded in a faith of the oppressed, must sustain the cultural congruity between Black life experiences and the systems through which those experiences are structured. The action, along with God's power working on behalf of and alongside the struggle for liberation, must address the comprehensive

---

87. Knoll, *One Nation Under God?*
88. Davis, *Slavery and Human Progress* and *The Problem of Slavery in Western Culture*.
89. Malcolm X interview with WUST, 1963.
90. Hooks, *Yearning*, 36–37.

system—prophetic engagement cannot analyze social condition absent from political practice and economic policy.[91]

Conclusion

There is no greater context in which to see the Black Church than its ordeal with slavery. The scourge of slavery birthed a spirituality to not only see God in the midst of oppressive conditions, but comprehend those troubling conditions as necessary to "get to glory." And, "if there were any associations of spirituality, Black churches were primarily about cathartic or emotional spirituality in which to appropriate issues like slavery and racism."[92] While true, this viewpoint is somewhat limiting as the aforementioned evolution of the Black Church demonstrates. But, the theological reality remains unchanged—God's image of community is primary and such a practice carries with it great costs and burdens, especially when faced with the affliction of American slavery.[93] The investigative process causes us to critically think about the role of pastoral leadership as we come to understand the Black Church. As it emerged from slavery, segregation, and Jim Crow, the guidance and direction provided by its leaders proved to position the Black Church as either accommodating, or prophetic, bringing to bear an argument of its resultant value: Does the Black Church preach a passive, docile doctrine that believes Christianity is "waiting on the Lord?" Or, does it teach an active, participatory approach that asserts Christianity as a willingness to "take one step and expect the Lord to make two?"

---

91. Cone, *A Black Theology of Liberation*.
92. Battle, *The Black Church in America*, 39.
93. Ibid.

Chapter Three

Contextual Shaping

Introduction

THE BLACK CHURCH HAS held a distinct position in the Black community. The position has been one of refuge, revolt, and in some cases, reform. As an institution, its standing in the community is undeniable, but accompanying that institutional standing is the high regard afforded the Black preacher/prophet. The traits and trends attributed to the Black Church can be directly traced to its leaders of the time. From the hopeful assurances and revolts through slavery, to the call for equal rights during legalized segregation, the preacher/prophet has been given a platform by the Black Church to speak out and stand up against injustice. And in so doing, according to Andrew Billingsley, the "leaders of Black antebellum churches stepped up to the challenges history had laid for them. And, because they acted, they helped to shape the course of history itself."[1]

In this chapter, I will initially draw upon Robert Franklin's concepts of pragmatic accommodationism and prophetic radicalism to interrogate the relationship between leadership philosophy and church practice. In addition, this process will use the 'fusion of horizon' theory of Hans-Georg Gadamer in an effort to correlate and interpret the leadership style, theory, and practice as they appear in the Black Church. It is with great scholarly trepidation that I attempt to make this connection, but I have no doubt that there is no better theory that captures the importance of connecting the history of the Black Church to its future.

---

1. Billingsley, *Mighty Like a River*, 67.

The Future Horizon for a Prophetic Tradition

Opiate versus Stimulant

For many, the link between religion and civil society is obvious. Historically, civic engagement of the Black Church has been well documented. Presently, media accounts regard civic engagement of Black ministers and churches as routine features of Black religious life. However, scholars over the years have differed sharply on the role that religion plays in Black civic engagement—some believe that the character of Black religiosity is heavenly-focused and acts as an opiate, while others assess Black religiosity as temporal and an inspiration.[2] The opiate perspective, which I liken to Franklin's "pragmatic accommodationism," insists that Black Christianity promotes a concentration on otherworldliness, functioning as an instrument of civic pacification and fatalism. The inspiration perspective, here likened to Franklin's "prophetic radicalism," makes the opposite claim, arguing that Black Christianity has played a central role in Black civic participation, catalyzing, for example, the collective involvement of Blacks in the modern civil rights movement. In either case, the emphasis falls on civic acquiescence versus civic agitation with the lingering question of relevance and usefulness.[3] Can the Black Church be, become, and maintain its relevance and usefulness without significant civic activity? The main European churches have been, until recently, state churches: leaders are formally confirmed, clergy paid, and schools subsidized by the state. Although rapidly changing in Scandinavian churches, religious doctrine is handed down by leaders—the pope, cardinals, and bishops in the Catholic Church—and the clergy's duty is to inculcate the members of the congregations in church dogma, and despite important differences in history, doctrine, and administration, the Anglican, Catholic, Lutheran, and Orthodox Churches of Europe have generally legitimated governmental authority and rallied popular support for their wars, laws, and other enterprises.[4] When these European churches came to the United States, they became voluntaristically-aligned with the cultural establishments that supported the state. This alignment with the cultural establishment left these churches less willing to be civic critics. In contrast, Black churches have always been independent of the state and often served as critics of state policy and advocates of individual rights. They played a

---

2. Nelsen and Nelson, *Black Church in the Sixties*, 14.

3. Acquiescence can resemble a kind of accommodationism, while agitation can promote a form of radicalism.

4. Lipset, *American Exceptionalism*.

leading role in attacking ethnic privilege in the United States and were the principal vehicles through which Black people were drawn into the process of reshaping American society created by a sense that the Black preacher was employed by the congregation rather than controlled by the cultural hegemony of the dominant structures. The result: action being informed by the needs, conditions and issues faced by the community and not imposed by motives, aims and desires of larger society.

Pragmatic Accommodationism

As Manning Marable has observed, "black religion is often viewed as the culprit, an agent of the oppressor, rather than a potentially liberating ideological force."[5] Pragmatic accommodationist theorists argue that religion works as a means of social control, offering Blacks a way to cope with personal and societal difficulties and thus undermining their willingness to actively challenge racial inequalities.[6] This perspective has prevailed across several generations of leading social scientists in a range of disciplines, including anthropology, psychology, sociology, and political science.[7] The theory has its origins in the writings of Karl Marx, who saw religion as an instrument of economic and political domination over 19th-century British workers. Marx famously dubbed religion as the "opium of the people."[8] By minimizing temporal concerns and encouraging believers to focus on other-worldly pursuits, religion, in his view, pacified oppressed groups so that they would accept their subordinated status in society.

Echoing Marx, Eugene Gordon, writing in the 1920s, accused Christianity of teaching Blacks to be "meek", "humble", and "to turn the other cheek when [they] should retaliate in kind." He further portrayed Negro Christianity as a "workable tool for others," and as "religiously enslaved"

---

5. Wilmore, *African American Religious Studies*, 333.

6. Baer, "Bibliography of Social Science Literature on Afro-American Religion in the United States," 413–30.

7. Powdermaker, *After Freedom*; Fauset, *Black Gods of the Metropolis*; Billings, "The Negro and His Church," 425–41; Dollard, *Caste and Class in a Southern Town*; Johnson, *Shadow of the Plantation*; Myrdal, *An American Dilemma*; Frazier and Lincoln, *The Negro Church in America*; Bunch, *The Political Status of the Negro in the Age of FDR*; Lane, *Political Life*.

8. Bottomore, *Karl Marx*.

with their minds neglecting "the very real and very present now for the delirious pleasure of wandering in a vague, remote, and uncertain hereafter."[9]

Social science research during the Jim Crow period reinforced the idea that Christianity subverted Black resistance. Political scientist Robert Lane concluded that religion offered urban Blacks and newly arrived immigrants an "otherworldly solace for temporal ills," which encouraged political apathy.[10] Although Gunnar Myrdal highlighted the Black Church's potential as a "power institution," he observed that the Black Church "has been relatively inefficient and uninfluential" as an instrument of collective action.[11] The harshest critique, however, was offered by sociologist E. Franklin Frazier who viewed the Black Church as "having cast an entire shadow over the entire intellectual life of Negroes" as well as being responsible for the "so-called backwardness" of Blacks.[12]

The first relevant attempt to resolve this question via survey research was sociologist Gary T. Marx's study of belief systems in the Black community.[13] More than any other study, Marx's findings sparked a debate between pragmatic accommodationism and prophetic radicalism prior to Franklin's articulation of the two terms.[14] In his 1964 metropolitan sample of Blacks, Marx found that intense religious belief had a contradictory effect relative to the aims of the civil rights movement. Specifically, Marx established that in his sample, the greater the subjective significance of religion to Black respondents, and the more often they attended church, the less militant their support of civil rights issues. Although Marx conceded that "many religious people are nevertheless militant," he concluded that until religion lost "its hold over these people, or comes to embody to a greater extent the belief that man as well as God can bring about secular change, and focuses more on the here and now," Black Christianity "would seem to be an important factor working against the widespread radicalization" of the Black public.[15]

More recently, Adolph Reed, in a critique of Jesse Jackson's 1984 presidential pursuit, sternly dismissed the idea that Black Christianity

---

9. Aptheker, *A Documentary History of the Negro People in the United States*.
10. Lane, *Political Life*, 250–55.
11. Myrdal, *An American Dilemma*, 873.
12. Frazier and Lincoln, *The Negro Church in America*, 90.
13. Marx, *Protest and Prejudice* and "Religion," 139–46.
14. Lincoln and Mamiya, *The Black Church in the African-American Experience*.
15. Marx, *Protest and Prejudice*, 105.

encourages civic engagement among adherents. Instead, he argued, Christianity encourages "political quietism" among Blacks, stifling the possibility of mass activism. Though he grudgingly acknowledged the Black Church's "tactical support of political mobilization," Reed maintained that Black Christianity is essentially an instrument of oppression, stating, "the domain of the black church has been the spiritual and institutional adaptation of Afro-Americans to an apparently inexorable context of subordination and dispossession.[16] Reed posits a fundamental tension between the Black Church and civic engagement, particularly because, in his opinion, the leadership of the Black Church is authoritarian and the tradition of the Black Church is antidemocratic—resting solely on the purpose, mission, and method identified and dictated by the pastor.

Prophetic Radicalism

The other side of the debate consists of theologians who contend that Black Christianity inspires and informs political liberation and activism.[17] Historians of American slavery have discovered that religion played a pivotal role in the survival and rebellion of African slaves.[18] Social scientists who have studied Black churches have highlighted the influence of Black pastoral leaders as catalysts for mobilizing Blacks into electoral and community politics.[19] Looking primarily at the civil rights-era in the South, sociologists have noted that the urban church, as an indigenous organization, provided the leadership base, social interaction, and communication networks required for collective action.[20]

Describing southern Blacks as a "God-fearing, churchgoing people," political scientists Donald Matthews and James Prothro maintained that the racially-segregated Black Church may have "planted the seeds for the destruction of segregation" by serving the political organizing needs of

16. Reed, Jr., *The Jesse Jackson Phenomenon*, 59.

17. Cone, *Black Theology and Black Power*; Cone, *A Black Theology of Liberation*; Harding, *There Is a River*; Paris, *The Social Teachings of the Black Churches*; West, *Prophesy Deliverance!*; West, *Prophetic Fragments*.

18. Genovese, *Roll, Jordan, Roll*; Raboteau, *Slave Religion*; Wilmore, *Black Religion and Black Radicalism*.

19. Hamilton, *The Black Preacher in America*; Childs, *The Political Black Minister*.

20. McAdam, *Political Process and Development of Black Insurgency*; Morris, *The Origins of the Civil Rights Movement*.

southern Blacks.[21] Their survey of Black and White southerners during the early years of the civil rights movement asked how often political campaigns were discussed at respondents' churches. While an overwhelmingly majority of both Blacks and Whites reported that political campaigns were not discussed in their church, 35% of Black respondents reported hearing some discussion about political campaigns, compared to only 18% of White respondents. Of those attending church services, 18% of Blacks reported that their pastor encouraged members to vote for a specific candidate, compared to only 5% of Whites. The investigators estimated that almost "a fifth of the Negroes who go to church thus receive direct clues as to how they should vote, and over a third hear some kind of discussion of elections."[22] These findings on direct church involvement in electoral politics during the civil rights movement, but prior to the passage of the 1965 Voting Rights Act, provide some evidence that southern Blacks were more amenable than their White counterparts to a civically-engaged church.

Matthews and Prothro's findings during the 1960s are comparable to patterns in contemporary politics. Katherine Tate's analysis of Black electoral behavior indicates that present-day religious institutions are an important organizational resource for disseminating information related to civic participation—elections, voter registration drives, providing a hub for individuals to volunteer with political candidates, as well as to give financial support to political campaigns.[23] Tate's findings confirm the enduring significance of religious institutions as a vehicle to mobilize Black civic participation in the post-civil rights era.

Multidimensional and Multifunctional

Political scientist Kenneth Wald begins to develop a multidimensional approach to the study of religion and civic participation by viewing religion as a "political resource." He explains that religious-based resources are "qualities possessed by religiously motivated people that can prove valuable in political action."[24] According to Wald, these qualities are represented in three types of religious-based resources for political mobilization—motivation, organization, and social interaction. Religious motivation could work

21. Matthews and Prothro, *Negroes and the New Southern Politics*, 232.
22. Ibid., 233.
23. Tate, "Black Political Participation," 1159–76.
24. Wald, *Religion and Politics in the United States*, 29.

in two ways. First, it could encourage political activism by fostering a sense of individual or collective empowerment—actors might feel that with spiritual guidance they could be effective in this-worldly pursuits, including politics. Second, religion might stimulate political action by leading participants to perceive political issues in moral terms. Religious leaders and political practitioners can articulate political issues, like immigration, as questions of morality, mobilizing religiously motivated actors for or against issues and for or against candidates who promote their moral perspective.

Wald also notes that religious ideals are potentially powerful sources of commitment and motivation that should not be underestimated as participatory resources. He believes that religious ideals inspire people to act politically because of a unique set of participatory incentives, making them so potentially powerful that "human beings will make enormous sacrifices if they believe themselves to be driven by a divine force."[25] Since these ideas are sacred to believers, they provide powerful cues for political engagement. Stephen Carter affirms, "people to whom religion truly matters, people who believe they have found answers to the ultimate questions, or are very close to finding them, will often respond to incentives other than those that motivate more secularized citizens."[26]

Black civic engagement takes on formal and informal connotations as it relates to civil processes. In this context "formal and informal" means that Blacks have been socialized into employing tactics that lie within and on the margins of mainstream civic processes. In other words, boycotting, picketing, and marching are just as legitimate tools of civic expression as are voting, canvassing neighborhoods, and letter writing campaigns. This mix of "formal and informal" institutionalized and organic behavior has deep roots in Black Church civic engagement. It evolved as a participatory norm following the collapse of Reconstruction and, depending on the opportunities for mobilization, has ebbed and flowed since that era.[27] While the exclusion of Blacks from the nation's civic and social life with the onset of Jim Crow cemented a racialized public sphere, these conditions also nurtured what political scientist Michael Dawson has referred to as a "black counterpublic."[28] This counterpublic, which included Black religious institutions, social movements, civil rights organizations, Black magazines

---

25. Ibid., 29–30.
26. Carter, *The Culture of Disbelief*, 275–76.
27. Nelsen, et al., *The Black Church in America*.
28. Dawson, "A Black Counterpublic?" 195–223.

and periodicals, social groups and clubs, etc., encouraged a variety of civic tactics and strategies that challenged White supremacist discourse and practice.[29]

Black civic engagement also differs in the level of commitment actors devote to civic action. Voting, for instance, takes relatively less effort than boycotting a store or organizing a neighborhood association. Taking part in a southern protest during the civil rights movement, for instance, required a greater level of personal commitment and risk than campaigning for a candidate in a northern city. Thus, religion's effect on Black civic engagement varies not only because of multidimensionality, but also because of the multifunctional nature and context of civic action.

Gadamer's Fusion of Horizons

Hans-Georg Gadamer's philosophical project sought to explore the phenomenon of understanding as it pertained to a *kind* of knowledge and truth that can be gained and transformed from multiple vantage points. Gadamer's attempt is not a methodology of the human sciences, "but an attempt to understand what the human sciences truly are, beyond their methodological self-consciousness, and what connects them with the totality of our experience of world."[30] Gadamer argued that individuals have a "historically-effected consciousness" that embeds them in a particular history and culture by which they are shaped. Thus, any interpretation involves a "fusion" of the object being interpreted and the background of the interpreter. In order for thought to be conscientious, Gadamer argues that it must become aware of anterior influences—habits of thought, language, environment, and experience.[31]

Gadamer further argues that to "acquire a horizon means that one learns to look beyond what is close at hand, not in order to look away from it, but to see it better, within a larger whole and in truer proportion."[32] This hermeneutical philosophy makes sense out of the way the Black Church views its sense of purpose—anticipating the future in light of the past. Gadamer maintains that while historical consciousness observes horizons of the past, hermeneutical consciousness merges the horizons of the past and present:

---

29. Usry and Keener, *Black Man's Religion*.
30. Gadamer, *Truth and Method*, xxii.
31. Ibid., xxiv.
32. Ibid., 304.

> Hence the horizon of the present cannot be formed without the past. There is no more an isolated horizon of the present in itself than there are historical horizons which have to be acquired. Rather, understanding is always the fusion of these horizons supposedly existing by themselves.[33]

Inasmuch as understanding is taken to involve "fusion of horizons," then it involves the formation of a new conceptual meaning that allows for integration. So what may be conceptualized as a true historical object, may in fact be recontextualized as a relationship which comprises both the reality of history and historical understanding in a contemporary context saturated with future implications. Reflecting a hermeneutical commitment to dialogue and engagement, Gadamer's philosophy can serve as a template to place the historicity of the Black Church in conversation with a prophetic reclamation—given, of course, his understanding that a fusion of present and past, old and new, is a continual growth that together makes something of living value while not explicitly distinguishing one apart from the other.[34]

Given that understanding always occurs against the background of experience, it just as much occurs on the basis of history. For Gadamer, understanding is an "effect" of history, while hermeneutical "consciousness" is itself that mode of being that is conscious of its own historical "being effected," so:

> In the process of understanding, a real fusing of horizons occurs—which means that as the historical horizon is projected, it is simultaneously superseded. To bring about this fusion in a regulated way is the task of what we called historically-effected consciousness."[35]

Awareness of the historically-effected character of understanding is, according to Gadamer, identical with an awareness of the hermeneutical situation and he also refers to that situation by means of the phenomenological concept of "horizon." Thus, understanding and interpretation always occur from within a particular "horizon" that results from a historically-determined situational location—meaning, "in a tradition this process of fusion is continually going on, for there old and new are always combining into

---

33. Ibid., 305.
34. Ibid.
35. Ibid., 306.

something of living value, without either being explicitly foregrounded from the other."[36]

Only in the past twenty years have scholars of African-American history, culture, and religion begun to identify that Black people created their own unique and distinctive forms of culture and worldview as parallel to, rather than replications of, the culture in which they were involuntary guests.[37] Consequently, a Black horizon of understanding is neither static nor unchanging, as understanding is not confined to the immediate horizon of its situation. Just as biases, preferences, and prejudices are brought into question in the process of understanding, so, in the encounter with another, is the horizon of our own understanding susceptible to change. For the Black Church, this took the form of varying degrees of emphases and valences in theological views—like the Old Testament notion of God as an avenging, conquering, liberating paladin, which remains a formidable anchor of faith in most Black churches.[38] The direct relationship between the holocaust of slavery, the notion of divine rescue, communal identity, and holistic scriptural application color the understandings of the Black Church in decisively implicit and explicit manners.

Gadamer views understanding as a matter of negotiation between oneself and one's partner in the hermeneutical dialogue, such that the process of understanding can be seen as a matter of coming to an "agreement:"

> [I]n being understood, the phenomena of historical life are seen as manifestations of universal life, of the divinity. Understanding and penetration mean, indeed, more than a human cognitive achievement and more than merely the creation of an inner universe.[39]

Coming to such an agreement means establishing a common framework or "horizon" and the result of such a process is the "fusion of horizons." This notion of a "horizon" means that every particular situation gains its meaning(s) only within its larger context.[40] Insofar as understanding is taken to involve a "fusion of horizons," the task also involves acquiring an appropriate historical horizon to form a new context of meaning that enables

---

36. Ibid., 305.
37. Lincoln and Mamiya, *The Black Church in the African-American Experience*, 2.
38. Ibid., 3.
39. Gadamer, *Truth and Method*, 208.
40. Ibid., 301.

integration of what is otherwise unfamiliar, strange, or anomalous.[41] In this respect, all understanding involves a process of mediation among two extremes and dialogue between polarities—where neither extreme remains unaffected. This leads us to adopt a "dialectical model" of the Black Church. Black churches are institutions undergoing a constant series of dialectical tensions involving polar opposites, constantly shifting between the polarities in historical time—priestly and prophetic, other-worldly and this-worldly, universalism and particularism, communal and personal, autocratic versus bureaucratic, resistance versus accommodation. While there is no Hegelian synthesis or ultimate resolution of the dialectic, the polarities give a comprehensive view of the complexity of Black churches as civic institutions, including their roles and functions in Black communities. The advantage of the dialectical model of the Black Church is that it leads to a more dynamic view of Black churches along a continuum of tensions, struggle, and change—thus assuring that the historical dynamism of institutions transitioning back-and-forth in response to certain issues or social conditions is not overlooked.[42] The most important aspect of both is the emphasis on constant interaction, the ongoing process of horizontal engagement which does not result in finality or complete elucidation.

In arguing that "historically-effected consciousness" exists and that it is shaped by, and embedded in, a particular history and culture, Gadamer conceptualized a mediational movement indispensable to understanding and arguing:

> [H]istorical consciousness fails to understand its own nature if, in order to understand, it seeks to exclude what alone makes understanding possible. To think historically means, in fact, to perform the transposition that the concepts of the past undergo when we try to think in them. To think historically always involves mediating between those ideas and one's own thinking.[43]

A disengaged observer cannot arrive at a fusion of horizons since the disengagement precludes the observer's horizon from taking part in the conversation. As the only stable and coherent institution to emerge from slavery, the Black Church was not only engaged, but immersed in Black civic life. While the social processes of migration, urbanization, and differentiation

41. Ibid., 302.
42. Lincoln and Mamiya, *The Black Church in the African-American Experience*, 11–16.
43. Gadamer, *Truth and Method*, 398.

had mitigating effects on this centrality and influence of the Black Church, the social gospel continued to inform and interact within the spheres of politics, economics, education, and other areas of civic life. Hence, the complexities of the Black Church as a civic institution require a more dynamic and integrative theory because it has played, and continues to play, more complex roles and assume more comprehensive burdens. Just as social class factors cannot be adequately applied to Black people without taking into account what Billingsley terms their "definition of the situation,"[44] in assessing the Black Church, one must consider what it has done before professing what it needs to do.

As slavery, segregation, and the high degree of racism in the United States began to reflect the difficulties in American society, the Black Church became the primary institution to carry the hopes and dreams of an outcast people. The enduring search for respect, acceptance, and equality marked the situational limit of one moment, yet provided the optimistic hope for another. In that regard, it was the Black Church that provided a transforming philosophy of knowledge and understanding through a reinterpretation of events stemming from an appropriation of scripture. Self-understanding is always realized only in the understanding of a subject matter, and that is what theology really says—that faith is just such an event, in which a new entity is found.[45] Gadamer helps us to see the error in viewing Blacks and Black institutions as merely being reactive to changes in larger society. A pro-Black, nationalist, historical perspective has correctly pointed out that American slaves were not automatons responding only to the conditions of the plantation system, but they were visionaries who formulated ideas about the possibilities of tomorrow—a heritage and creative impulse directly resulting from the transformative philosophy and practice of the Black Church.[46]

For most Whites during slavery, Christianity contained an aspect of control, intended to produce obedient and docile slaves. Speaking metaphorically, horizons can provide perspective by being the implicit and explicit beliefs that contextualize understanding. By establishing what is relevant and irrelevant, horizons mark the boundaries of comprehension as background beliefs and knowledge affect what and how something is understood. If taken as the beliefs that make understanding possible, one can

---

44. Billingsley, *Black Families in White America*.
45. Linge, *Philosophical Hermeneutics*.
46. Lincoln and Mamiya, *The Black Church in the African-American Experience*, 195.

view Gadamer's fusion of horizons as the manner in which the context of a subject can be weighted and interpreted differently from what was initially perceived. Thus, the mountains of slavery, oppression, segregation, and racism become moveable, not immutable. Negro spirituals like "Come This Far by Faith" and marching slogans such as "We Shall Overcome" provide a new horizon—or at the very least, a different hermeneutic—that then offers a new understanding.

For Gadamer, understanding is essentially open, and thereby also a risk. The tentative nature of understanding is unsettling because it involves anticipation and experience, both of which come with prejudice, and require temporal distance to distinguish the true prejudices, by which we understand, from the false, by which we misunderstand.[47] Hence, a newly-constructed hermeneutic for the Black Church will include historical consciousness and make conscious the prejudices governing its present understanding. For Gadamer:

> Real historical thinking must take into account of its own historicity. Only then will it cease to chase the phantom of a historical object that is the object of progressive research, and learn to view the object as the counterpart of itself and hence understand both. The true historical object is not an object at all, but the unity of the one and the other, a relationship that constitutes both the reality of history and the reality of historical understanding.[48]

Thus, through the foregrounding of prejudices and suspension of judgments, the logical structure of a question is presented whose essence is to open up possibilities and keep them open. Most experience, true experience specifically, that delivers insight is negative, drawing from this the conclusion that true experience must thus lead to openness to newer experience. Gadamer's Socratic wisdom clearly finds expression in this hope that the insight in the prejudiced character and negativity of hermeneutic understanding can only lead to further openness.[49]

Openness rather than closure provides a hermeneutic situation for the Black Church, and therefore, it can never transcend the realm of prejudices, but it can transcend those that have proven inept or ineffective. How does the Black Church go about this? Gadamer counsels against seeking quick fixes because this would only be a delusion fostered by the era, expectation,

---

47. Gadamer, *Truth and Method*, 298.
48. Ibid., 299.
49. Grondin, "Gadamer's Basic Understanding of Understanding," 36–51.

and effort. The Black Church must learn to work through shared experience, as it is often shared experience that allows recognition of what is appropriate, purposeful, meaningful, and necessary.[50] On the eve of his assassination, Dr. King apocalyptically announced,

> . . . if I were standing at the beginning of time, with the possibility of general and panoramic view of the whole human history up to now, and the Almighty said to me, "Martin Luther King, which age would you like to live in?"—I would take my mental flight by Egypt through, or rather across the Red Sea, through the wilderness on toward the promised land. And in spite of its magnificence, I wouldn't stop there. I would move on by Greece, and take my mind to Mount Olympus. And I would see Plato, Aristotle, Socrates, Euripides, and Aristophanes assembled around the Parthenon as they discussed the great and eternal issues of reality. But I wouldn't stop there. I would go on, even to the great heyday of the Roman Empire. And I would see developments around there, through the various emperors and leaders. But I wouldn't stop there. I would even come up to the day of the Renaissance, and get a quick picture of all that the Renaissance did for the cultural and esthetic life of man. But I wouldn't stop there. I would even go by the way that the man for whom I'm named had his habitat. And I would watch Martin Luther as he tacked his ninety-five theses on the door at the church in Wittenberg. But I wouldn't stop there. I would come on up even to 1863, and watch a vacillating president by the name of Abraham Lincoln finally come to the conclusion that he had to sign the Emancipation Proclamation. But I wouldn't stop there. I would even come up to the early thirties, and see a man grappling with the problems of the bankruptcy of his nation. And come with the eloquent cry that we have nothing to fear but fear itself. But I wouldn't stop there. Strangely enough, I would turn to the Almighty, and say, "If you allow me to live just a few years in the second half of the twentieth century, I will be happy."[51]

The hermeneutical situation highlights the manner in which we are thrust into a history or set of stories that we did not begin and cannot end, but which we must continue in one way or another.[52] The action, therefore, must have a strategic focus and direction, as well as an accountability to keep moving toward a goal because without these elements, interest

---

50. Ibid.
51. Washington, *A Testament of Hope*, 279–80.
52. Heidegger, *Being and Time*.

is soonlost and action wasted.[53] So in determining how to act, the Black Church must possess a comprehension of itself as well as the unfolding narrative in which it finds itself—thus, if it has to act, it has to understand, for better or worse, who and where it is and who and where it wants to be. From the beginning then, it is involved in the practical task of deciphering the narrative of which it is a part so that it can know how to move forward.[54]

In the hermeneutical situation the actions we take also react back upon our action-oriented understanding. They become part of what we understand when we understand our past and ourselves, as well as part of how we anticipate our future. So, not only are we constantly navigating the narrative of which we are a part so that we know how to move forward, but also we are always already in the process of moving forward. In this regard, the Black Church's present understanding of these stories is an understanding from the middle of an ongoing narrative with the future still outstanding.[55] It has to reflect on and understand itself in the process of continuing to live and act as it has already understood itself. In other words, the Black Church lives or writes its narrative according to the meanings it has possessed and understands those meanings according to the ways it continues to live and write its narrative.[56] Taken in this manner, Gadamer's account for the Black Church's hermeneutical situation has important implications for civil society. If it attempts to understand itself and to consider how it ought to act proceeding only on the constantly shifting ground of an ongoing history, it cannot hope to transcend that history. To combat this, Gadamer offers an institutional ethic that can accommodate a human nature and reason that is also historical.[57]

Gadamer's hermeneutical use of "horizon" and "fusion" presents a useful inroad to understanding the historical Black Church as it moves forward. Horizon, in his sense, is the larger context of meaning in which the Black Church is set. The horizon is a never completed, situated awareness that provides a limited range of vision at any given time, and allows the horizon of the present and the horizon of the past to converge in a hermeneutical circle. This circle can be wrongly thought of as a circular track of question and answer where the horizons are discrete poles instead

---

53. Franklin, *Crisis in the Village*, 23.
54. Warnke, "Hermeneutics, Ethics, and Politics," 79–101.
55. Gadamer, *Truth and Method*, 180–83.
56. Warnke, "Hermeneutics, Ethics, and Politics," 79–101.
57. Gadamer, *Truth and Method*, 310–12.

of a "contextually fulfilled circle" which joins the horizons of the Black Church into "a processual whole."[58] As a result, the horizons are always and intimately bound with the interactive engagement occurring in the sphere of shared context. Thus the horizons and interactive engagement are comprised in a closed circuit of shared influence where the past that situates the present is changed when engaged and in turn transforms again the context of the present. Neither horizon can be viewed as static or isolated from the other. Bounded by a bond of tradition, the "fusion" does not bring together two dislocated phenomena, but revisits and revises the related two horizons through engagement. "Fusion" therefore stands as a process of historical adaptation and contemporary application, making it a constructive alternative to pragmatic accommodationism.

Leadership, Change Theory, and Networked Organization

According to Ronald Heifetz and Marty Linsky, leadership would be a safe undertaking if organizations and communities only faced problems for which they already have the solutions.[59] This is a critical lens through which to view the Black Church. Heifetz and Linsky distinguish *technical* challenges, those which people have the necessary know-how and procedures to tackle, from *adaptive* challenges, those that require experiments, new discoveries, and adjustments from numerous places within the organization or community.[60] As adaptive challenges present themselves, the tendency is for members of an organization, particularly the Black Church, to look to an expert, specifically the pastor, to provide a technical solution—thus, running the risk of dysfunction, dissatisfaction, and dissolution. "For this reason," Heifetz and Linsky assert, "people often try to avoid the dangers, either consciously or subconsciously, by treating an adaptive challenge as if it were a technical one." Which is why, the two conclude, routine management is more prevalent than leadership.[61]

To define leadership as an activity that addresses adaptive challenges not only considers the values that a goal represents, "but also the goal's ability to mobilize people to face, rather than avoid, tough realities and conflicts."[62]

58. Gadamer, "The Problem of Historical Consciousness," 103–62.
59. Heifetz and Linsky, *Leadership on the Line*, 13.
60. Ibid.
61. Ibid., 14.
62. Heifetz, *Leadership without Easy Answers*, 23.

The most difficult and valuable task of pastoral leadership may be advancing goals and articulating strategies that promote adaptive solutions. The role of leadership is to undertake an iterative process of back-and-forth between the balcony and the dance floor, obtaining a clearer view of reality and big-picture perspective while simultaneously being immersed in the action.[63]

The assertions of Heifetz and Linsky suggest that, in reference to the Black Church, pastoral leaders would not only have to be conscious about the challenges facing the Church and community, but careful to interpret those challenges in adaptive terms as well. If, as Barbara Crosby and John Bryson argue, that in order to "coordinate action and make headway on resolving a complex public problem, the organizations involved need to be aware of the whole problem system and recognize that it has to undergo significant change,"[64] then evaluating and engaging the broad scope of systems, structures, and policies affecting the external community would be essential.

Additionally, the internal challenges facing the Black Church require a multi-tiered process that addresses the various dimensions collectively. For instance, theological reflection on mission, identity, and purpose would need to accompany careful attention to contextual realities, both relying heavily on the Church's theological heritage and confronting the current social, economic, and political situation. As one pastor who was interviewed mentioned, "the clues will have to come from the pews." Translation—moving forward, community and congregation members must have an active role in any effort of the Black Church's reclamation of its prophetic position because they are the ones immersed in the social, economic, and political conditions. Yet throughout this process, a clear focus on stewardship and partnership must be maintained to avoid the Church's prior pitfalls of accommodationism, isolation, and dysfunction. John P. Kotter explains that "needed change can still stall because of inwardly focused cultures, paralyzing bureaucracy, parochial politics, a low level of trust, lack of teamwork, arrogant attitudes . . . and the general human fear of the unknown."[65]

Given the pattern of accommodationism currently, it would be prudent for the Black Church to mirror the manner in which change actually occurs in organizations. Traditional strategic planning processes, in which an identified "upper" management team creates a plan with a set of "S.M.A.R.T." goals—specific, measurable, achievable, realistic,

---

63. Heifetz and Linsky, *Leadership on the Line*, 53.
64. Crosby and Bryson, *Leadership for the Common Good*, 9.
65. Kotter, *Leading Change*, 20.

time-framed—and then systematically disseminates it into the system for implementation tend to incorporate linear methods to obtain complex, dynamic outcomes. Since, according to Kotter, attempting to create major change with simple, linear, analytical processes almost always fails,[66] *situational management* must be replaced with *directional leadership*. Within voluntary organizations such as the church, it is very difficult—arguably impossible—to enforce change from the pulpit without pushback from the pew. In the case of the Black Church, the history of grassroots mobilization and liberal democratic leadership embodied in many of its internal and external practices suggests that a traditional approach to change will be unsuccessful because it inadequately engages the grassroots.

John Kotter defines management as a set of processes that can keep a complicated system running smoothly, whereas leadership is a set of processes that create or adapt organizations to significantly changing circumstances.[67] Unfortunately for the Black Church, a management emphasis has been institutionalized, resulting in a culture that discourages pastors from learning *how* to lead. Ironically, this institutionalization is a direct result of past successes and hence the repetitious pattern of "doing what's always been done." Kotter diagnoses the syndrome as follows:

> Success creates some degree of market dominance, which in turn produces growth. After a while, keeping the ever-larger organization under control becomes the primary challenge. So attention turns inward, and managerial competencies are nurtured. With a strong emphasis on management but not leadership, bureaucracy and an inward focus take over. But with continued success, the result mostly of market dominance, the problem often goes unaddressed and an unhealthy arrogance begins to evolve. All of these characteristics then make any transformation effort much more difficult.[68]

The combination of organizations that resist change and managers who have not been taught how to create change is lethal, particularly because sources of complacency are rarely adequately addressed since urgency is not an issue for managers, masquerading as leaders, who have been asked to simply maintain a current system of practices.[69]

---

66. Ibid., 25.
67. Ibid., 25.
68. Ibid., 27.
69. Ibid., 29.

For Christians, there are even more fundamental theological reasons to target a holistic approach for change. First, we begin with our realization that Jesus always involved the disciples in His ministerial work—a dynamic collaborative of community and shared responsibility. Whether through actual "hands-on" participation, cognitive enlightening, or spiritual awakening, a simple developmental aspect of Jesus' leadership was to model a practice from which the disciples could move the ministry forward following His ascension.[70] This pervasive theme, referred to by John Howard Yoder as participation or correspondence, is where "the believer's behavior or attitude is said to correspond to or reflect or partake of the same quality or nature as that of the Lord."[71]

Second, social, economic, and political factors shaped ministry. In general, the social setting of Jesus' ministry was characterized by a pronounced cultural divide—in particular classism, capitalism and colonialism. In several instances in the Synoptic Gospels, Jesus specifically addresses the spiritual and psychological toll on the community caused by the elitism and arrogance of the priests and city dwellers.[72] The presence of poverty is deeply reflected throughout Jesus' ministry: Judas complained that the cost of the expensive perfume used to anoint Jesus' feet should have been "given to the poor;"[73] the Roman tax structure was such a significant issue that the Pharisees used it in an attempt to trap Jesus;[74] and the suffering that the Roman colonial presence visited on the Jewish people was so prevalent and brutal that its influence on the political consciousness of Jesus is inescapable—it must not be lost that while He was worshiped as the Son of God, His earthly time was also spent as an oppressed Roman colonial subject. In fact, the priests' political quietism and accommodation of Roman policies made Jesus' stance against them unquestionably political in nature.[75]

Third, an interactive, interdependent understanding of the Trinity points toward a dynamic, communal approach to leadership and change. If, according to Leonardo Boff, the Spirit of God is the power of the new and of a renewal in all things, the memory of Jesus' deeds and words with a mission to liberate the oppressed, as well as the principle that creates differences and

---

70. See John 14:12
71. Yoder, *The Politics of Jesus*, 113.
72. Luke 6:20
73. John 12:4–5
74. Matthew 22:17
75. Hendricks, Jr., *The Politics of Jesus*.

communion, then one could agree that the Spirit is the originator of differences and instigator of communion seeking to strengthen the community in working to fulfill its needs.[76] Thus, the many expressions of vitality and services in the community are not a threat to unity, but an opportunity for all to be enriched because communion does not suppress or reduce differences, but integrates them into the purpose of the common good.[77] Leadership, therefore, becomes a relational practice that places those who lead and those who follow in a mutually-empowering dynamic, one that calls on the Spirit for creativity and innovation, and never in an individualistic sense or for self-advancement.

Finally, targeting a holistic approach for change is consistent with a key Christian tenet—liberation. As Gustavo Gutierrez reminds, the proper understanding of history is one in which the human being is seen as assuming conscious responsibility for human destiny, yet Jesus Christ liberates humanity from sin, which is the root of all disruption of love, justice, and community.[78] The liberating Spirit of God gives the Black Church a future horizon working in present circumstances toward God's missional and ecclesial purposes for the Church and all of creation. Since leadership and change address the future, liberation must be at the core of any approach because it was this quest that birthed, nurtured, and sustained the Black Church and community through times of social inequality, economic disparity, and political perfidy. The biblical narrative challenges the Black Church, and Christians as a whole, to take part in God's unfolding action in the world—an eschatological definition identified with hope that gives rise to a critical, prophetic voice—fostering an activist, liberative, and revolutionary stance grounded on faith in God.[79]

The liberation premise, which ascribes the message of the prophets to justice and describes the mission of Jesus as a revolution,[80] is a biblical

---

76. Boff, *Trinity and Society*, 192–95.

77. Ibid., 196.

78. Gutierrez, *A Theology of Liberation*.

79. An older eschatological focus did not blossom into a social, economic, and political framework. While eschatology had been a prime concern of theologians since the start of the 20th century, it had been apolitical—private, individual, and in existential terms. With the advent of a social gospel, eschatology was given a historical, collective, and future-directed orientation. Moltmann, *Theology of Hope*; Metz, *Theology of the World*; Gollwitzer, *The Christian Faith and the Marxist Criticism of Religion*; Cone, *A Black Theology of Liberation*.

80. Isaiah 61:1, Matthew 10:34

interpretation of a call to action whose principal methodological innovation was to view theology from the perspective of the poor and the oppressed. This means that systemic practices and institutional policies should be called into question, challenged, critiqued, and corrected as they relate to creating and perpetuating a marginalized, minimized, and disenfranchised segment of society. This emphasis on praxis over doctrine defines a position that advocates a circular relationship between orthopraxis and orthodoxy—seeing the two as having a symbiotic relationship. Liberation, therefore, contradicts a politically-docetic interpretation of scripture which leaves oppressive structures unchallenged and thus abdicates Christian responsibility to wage struggle against contextual realities. This misconception can be traced to two crucial developments: first, Paul's transformation of Jesus' concern for collective social, economic, and political deliverance into an obsession with individual personal piety; and second, Constantine's transmutation of a radical faith of the oppressed founded upon Jesus' teachings to the official, militaristic religion of the oppressor.[81]

Coupled with being more reactive than proactive (or, practicing situational management versus directional leadership), another common error made by the Black Church is to pursue change from an individualistic, isolated silo versus a larger, integrative collaborative. Crosby and Bryson distinguish two types of organizations: the in-charge organization and the networked organization (see Figure 2.1). The in-charge organization has at the apex, an individual or small group that establishes organizational direction, determines guiding policies, and transmits directives downward. Embedded in this ideal type is the assumption that the organization engages in highly rational, expert-based planning and decision making to address issues. Arguing the inadequacy of this structure in today's interconnected and interdependent world, they see a networked organization which is a part of a variety of external networks that are fluid and chaotic as a better, more beneficial model to influence change.[82] As Crosby and Bryson point out,

> change advocates have to engage in political, issue-oriented, and therefore messy planning and decision making, in which shared goals and mission are being developed as the process moves along. New networks must be created, old ones coopted or neutralized. These networks range from the highly informal, in which the main

---

81. Hendricks, *The Politics of Jesus*.
82. Crosby and Bryson, *Leadership for the Common Good*, 5.

activity is information sharing, to more organized shared-power arrangements.[83]

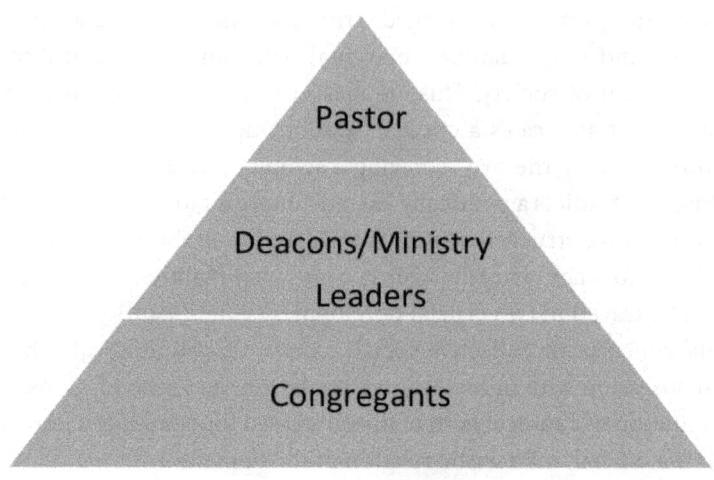

An "In-Charge" Organization

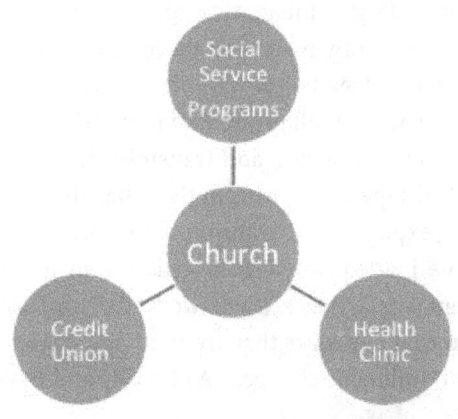

A "Networked" Organization

Figure 2.1: Hierarchical and Networked Organizations

In order for the networked model to be effective, two premises must be accepted. First, a certain loss of autonomy will be experienced. The Black

83. Ibid., 9.

Church and its leadership have historically served as the primary source of solutions for the Black community. From food shelves to clothing drives, what may not have been formal, integrative processes were in fact informal, institutional practices that addressed needs in the community. From the time of their birth up to the present, Black churches have stood in their respective communities as symbols of independence from White domination, subtly transmitting by their ubiquitous presence, a spirit of dignity and self-respect. Consequently, as Peter Paris points out, the principle of autonomy and its impact on the Black community are deeply rooted in religious, moral, and political values.[84] But, from the Black Church perspective, while it may have had the connection to the community, it lacked access to the resources of the wider community to effect systemic change. Within a networked model, the wider community may possess the resources and know-how, but lack the trust from, and relationship with, the Black Church and community. Here, what Geoffrey Vickers calls "acts of appreciation," becomes a useful lens because appreciation merges judgment of what is *real* with judgment of what is *valuable*. Identifying problems involves new appreciation of how something works, what is wrong with it, and how it might become better—this "appreciation subsequently shapes the way a public problem is defined, the solutions considered, and the accommodation of stakeholders' interests."[85]

Second, an understanding of culture is pivotal. Edgar Schein distinguishes three levels of organizational culture: artifacts, which are visible organizational structures and processes; espoused beliefs and values, which are strategies, goals and philosophies; and underlying assumptions, which are unconscious, taken-for-granted beliefs, perceptions, thoughts, and feelings.[86] The culture of the Black Church is inextricably linked to the historical condition, treatment, and needs of the Black community. A non-acceptance of this interrelationship will undermine the efforts of any network with which it becomes involved. As Schein points out:

> The most central issue for leaders, therefore, is how to get at the deeper levels of a culture, how to assess the functionality of the assumptions made at that level, and how to deal with the anxiety that is unleashed when those levels are challenged.[87]

84. Paris, "The Public Role of the Black Churches."
85. Crosby and Bryson, *Leadership for the Common Good*, 15.
86. Schein, *Organizational Culture and Leadership*, 26.
87. Ibid., 37.

Schein defines culture as "a pattern of shared basic assumptions that was learned by a group as it solved its problems of external adaptation and internal integration, that has worked well enough to be considered valid and, therefore, to be taught to new members as the correct way to perceive, think, and feel in relation to those problems."[88] Given this definition, one can see not just the historical connection between Black Church culture and leadership, but also the problem posed by a networked model—any challenging or questioning of basic, underlying assumptions will release anxiety and defensiveness.[89]

For purposes here, the use of *"culture"* builds on Raymond Williams' notion of culture "as the study of relationships between elements in a whole way of life."[90] On the basis of the cultural lifestyles of the Black community—from slavery to emancipation, and ideally from emancipation to liberation—I adopt Dwight Hopkins' modification of Williams' definition:

> Culture is always religious insofar as the way of life of all human beings entails some yearning for, belief in, and ritualization around that which is ultimate—that which is both part of and greater than the self. Culture is religious because the ultimate concern is both present in cultural material and transcends it.[91]

Conclusion

I have woven together Franklin's leadership characterizations with organizational theory and principles, the purpose of which is to convey that while Black Church leadership differs in perspective, content, and style from the Western theological tradition, its affirmation enabled Black people to experience another definition of their humanity:[92]

> In the context of a society structured as a racial hierarchy, those who shared "European" features controlled political and economic power and used it for the benefit of their community. The Black

---

88. Ibid., 17.
89. Ibid., 32.
90. Williams, *The Long Revolution*, 63.
91. Hopkins, "Self (Co)Constitution.
92. Cone, *God of the Oppressed*, 3.

Church emerged as one of the only communities Europeans could not control.[93]

Coupled with its independence, came the autonomy and control offered to the Black preacher that served as a training ground to learn and cultivate traits necessary for leadership in a Black context. Gadamer's 'fusion of horizons' encourages the Black Church to use its past to inform its present and future in a critical manner that confronts brutal facts and continually refine its path.[94] A drawback to the autonomy and control is the identification with the leader opposed to the mission, to which Jim Collins warns,

> [T]he moment a leader allows himself to become the primary reality people worry about, rather than reality being the primary reality, you have a recipe for mediocrity, or worse. This is one of the key reasons why less charismatic leaders often produce better long-term results than their charismatic counterparts.[95]

The Black Church is a complex organization but not a typical bureaucracy—behavior and processes are organized, but not highly formalized. A striking feature of the Black Church is the considerable loyalty and commitment displayed by church members toward their pastor, as demonstrated by the "spontaneous" outpouring of cash to Bishop Eddie Long during a recent worship service. Positively and negatively, the relationship between the pastor and members is often one of charismatic leader to followers rather than the formalized levels of command practiced by corporations, or White churches. This proves to be pivotal if the Black Church is to claim a relevant position on the future horizon.

---

93. Battle, *The Black Church in America*, 29.
94. Collins, *Good to Great*, 69–70.
95. Ibid., 72.

Chapter Four

Moving Forward

Introduction

THIS UNDERTAKING WAS AN attempt to historicize and contextualize the Black Church with the hope of reclaiming and recontextualizing its social gospel dimensions, which cannot be adequately addressed without first identifying the mutual enhancement that Black Church civic engagement and missional ecclesiology provide for one another. Given that organizations tend to become microcosms of the larger culture, the recognition of historical, practical, contextual, relational, and educational components relative to community is essential to the future relevance of the Black Church. Religious practices, discussions about the role of the Negro/Black Church, and Black cultural images have repeatedly come together in important ways, not least in their impact on the real conditions of Blacks in the nation.[1] As a result, identifying the social gospel dimensions of the historic Black Church that can be reclaimed and recontextualized for renewed civic engagement provides insight into the functional shift awaiting the Black Church as well as the implications for the larger Church-wide community.

Based on research findings that revealed high levels of intentional conversations, strong connection between congregation and community needs, in addition to the consistent recognition of the critical role of pastoral leadership, seminary education, and partnerships, I conclude there are three areas that will help the Black Church effectively renew its prophetic

---

1. Evans, *The Burden of Black Religion*, 10.

engagement within civil society. First, a repurposed understanding of Black issues that has been lost due to social power dynamics within Black culture; second, a reformed practical approach to leadership education and training; and third, a recontextualized relational model for partnerships.

Generating Systemic Energy

I claim there are four areas that can generate the necessary systemic energy for the Black Church as an institution to create and effect social, political, and economic change. Diane Lane argues that many "would be correct in asserting that the worst thing that ever happened to Black Americans in the twentieth century was the success of the Civil Rights Movement."[2] This assessment comes close to my argument for reclamation and recontextualization as in less than forty years, we have witnessed a vibrant and active Black Church, in all of its myriad expressions with a focus on education, capacity-building, and elevation of race, become, for too many, a place of hopelessness and despair.[3] I begin this chapter by moving from a historical perspective to what I believe is a new conception of what it means to be, and become, the Black Church. Throughout this chapter, I plan to weave together five components—historical, practical, contextual, relational, educational—into four areas of focus: intergenerational compatibility, power dynamics, leadership education and training, and partnerships.

In its ever-increasing multi-cultural and diverse context, the church in the United States of America is in decline and in crisis. The decline and crisis can be directly attributed to two factors: a Eurocentric-theology presented as normative and blindness to the oppressive practices that systematize, syncretize, and support that normative presentation. It is clearly evident that Western mission has "been very much a European-church-centered enterprise," the subtle assumption of many being "that the church's missionary mandate lay not only in forming the church of Jesus Christ, but in shaping the Christian communities that it birthed in the image of the church of western European culture."[4] A reorientation of theological understanding that includes context and culture, as well as reflection and action, serves as a contributory channel for Black Church civic engagement and missional ecclesiology.

2. Hayes, "Movin' on up a Little Higher," 14.
3. Ibid.
4. Guder, *Missional Church*, 4.

As we begin to envision the church of Jesus Christ not as the purpose or goal of the Christian gospel, but rather as its instrument and witness, the context and culture of the Black Church adds to missional ecclesiology the premise that there is no mission without critical reflection and interrogative action. Without reflection and action, missional ecclesiology is reduced to a self-focused, institutional maintenance and enhancement effort with no engagement with social institutions, systems and structures that affect God's creation:

> Mission is not just a program of the church. It defines the church as God's sent people. Either we are defined by mission, or we reduce the scope of the gospel and the mandate of the church ... The doctrine of the church, ecclesiology, can and is still taught with little or no reference to the church's missionary vocation.[5]

In order to avoid the dominant cultural experience becoming oppressive, exclusionary, and even racist, the infusion of Black Church civic engagement as reflective and active define a missionary people "whose witness will prophetically challenge precisely those dominant patterns as the church accepts its vocation to be an alternative community. The structures of leadership and community life must then carry through that prophetic vocation."[6]

For the church to address its missional and ecclesial identity, it must carefully include the multiple cultural contexts that it seeks to enter, share, and shape because it will be shaped by those contexts "just as it will constantly challenge and shape" them. Such a calling never leaves the church in a finished, settled, or permanent position, but rather, a "dynamic interaction between the gospel and all human cultures" that always "lies at the heart of what it means to be the church."[7] An authentic missional ecclesiology equips the church to engage the cultural realities for Kingdom advancement, and the Black Church offers a spiritual principle, perspective, and platform from which that can be done—a biblical understanding that incorporates liberation and reconciliation as components of mission. According to James Cone, to "understand the biblical view of reconciliation, we must see it in relation to the struggle of freedom in an oppressed society. In America, that means seeing reconciliation in the social context of black

---

5. Ibid., 6–7.
6. Ibid., 10.
7. Ibid., 14–15.

liberation."[8] Missional ecclesiology, therefore, in a social context of cultural and racial oppression, must not be afraid to critically reflect and systemically act in regard to inclusive practices of the church. Or, in the words of Cone, ask the hard questions and have the difficult conversations.[9]

Intergenerational Compatibility

Can the Black Church be relevant to generations who know only of its foundational context through secondhand storytelling and history books? This fundamental question needs to take into account the inherent element of the Black Church and its continued focus on the historical context in which it was formed, which, according to womanist theologian Brandee Jasmine Mimitzraiem, makes it difficult for those who did not experience that context to locate themselves in, and relate themselves with, the institution.[10] The lack of historical knowledge, familiarity, and identification is far too often viewed as a problem with the "younger generation" who neither knows nor understands "how things used to be." It is clear, however, that younger generations only know what has been traditionally passed down. And, if the Black Church is to become future-relevant, it has to approach missional ecclesiology as an intergenerational discipline, practice, and purpose.

The Black Church as the ideological institution to address Black struggles should be both relevant to and receptive of younger generations. This has not happened. Perhaps, as Mimitzraiem argues, because the Black Church has not been made to see that the experiences of the younger generations "are valid sources for theology."[11] Their validity, however, is unquestionable. As Hopkins writes, the younger generation, on the one hand, has sought to pursue the older generation's pioneering agenda, and on the other hand, has claimed its own distinct approaches. So, the younger generation is both an heir and harbinger of the Black Church.[12] Ironically, it was social, political, and economic discomfort and disenchantment from which the Black Church rose and an unwillingness to address the conditional experiences of Blacks that cultivated its growth, significance, and

8. Cone, *God of the Oppressed*, 207–08.
9. Ibid., 208.
10. Mimitzraiem, "Too Young to Be Black," 334.
11. Ibid., 346.
12. Hopkins, *Introducing Black Theology of Liberation*, 88.

status. So, it is not surprising that the younger generation's inclusion and infusion of issues such as Afrocentricity, gender discrepancies, and social inequities provide an opportunity for intergenerational compatibility as the struggles of the younger generation is a result of the historical Black experience in America. In short, the younger generation has grown up dealing with the advances, consequences, and implications of the 1960s and 1970s liberation movements led by the Black Church.[13]

The younger generation is conscious of, and definitely not callous about, its history. This presents an obstacle and an opportunity for the Black Church—the lived realities of the Black Church represent the historical sources of the younger generation. However, the caution for the Black Church is not to make history primary over and against the experiences of the younger generation. The worth and value of the Black Church to the Black community is undeniable and unprecedented, giving it a choice according to Mimitzraiem: either assume that the Civil Rights and Black Power Movements had no effect whatsoever or acknowledge that the Black experience has changed since the 1960s.[14] The Black Church has the responsibility to negotiate between generations—it is the resource that maintains the language of historical tradition and the legacy of radical transformation. The missional ecclesiology of the Black Church is a theology of praxis, not of passivity. Therefore, a focused approach of praxis, as well as context, relative to bridging the generations serves as a foundational framework for the Black Church moving forward.

Praxis & Context

In *Models of Contextual Theology*, Stephan B. Bevans puts forth a praxis model of contextual theology that focuses on Christian identity "within a context particularly as that context is understood in terms of social change."[15] According to Bevans, the praxis model

> is a never-ending process that gets its considerable power from the recognition that God manifests God's presence not only, or perhaps not even primarily, in the fabric of culture, but also and perhaps principally in the fabric of history. [It] is a way of doing theology that is formed by knowledge at its most intense level—the

13. Mimitzraiem, "Too Young to Be Black," 337–47.
14. Ibid., 361.
15. Bevans, *Models of Contextual Theology*, 70.

level of reflective action. It is also about discerning the meaning and contributing to the course of social change, and so it takes its inspiration from neither classic texts nor classic behavior but from present realities and future possibilities.[16]

The praxis model can be traced to the prophetic tradition that grounded the civic engagement of the Black Church,[17] the New Testament dictum to not only be a hearer of the word but a doer as well,[18] and the close connection of ethical behavior with theological thought.[19] So, to speak of the praxis model, I am articulating a model "the central insight of which is that theology is done not simply by providing relevant expressions of Christian faith, but also by a commitment to Christian action."[20] But even more than this, I am suggesting that theology must be understood as the product of continual dialogue between two aspects of Christian life—missional ecclesiology and civic engagement.

All theology is contextual, which is to say that all theology is grounded in the very hearts, hands, and minds of those believing, living, and laboring; and there is no theology that is, or can be, set apart or distanced from culture, heritage, or tradition.[21] But, any context can be, or become, perverted and in need of liberation and reconciliation. However, context, as a human construct and humanizing product, posits culture, albeit varied, as essentially good. The church, as a context, might express a high degree of satisfaction with the spread of its beliefs, traditions, and customs, but as it reflects on the manner and practices in which they were and continue to be done, it might become "more and more convinced of the perversion of U.S. American individualism and the need for a greater sense and exercise of community."[22] The rereading of the gospel and reapplication of the Christian tradition within this context, coupled with continual, communal reflection on ways to develop more of a cultural-communal sense, might produce a more challenging brand of missional ecclesiology.

---

16. Ibid.
17. Isaiah 6; Amos 1–5.
18. James 1:22; 2:17
19. Augustine and Aquinas argued that faith informed behavior through a rational process that sought happiness, virtue, and the highest good.
20. Bevans, *Models of Contextual Theology*, 72.
21. Hayes, "Movin' on up a Little Higher," 17.
22. Bevans, *Models of Contextual Theology*, 75.

The Future Horizon for a Prophetic Tradition

What Does This Mean for the Black Church?

Just as Du Bois insisted that the time had come for "the Negro Church" to divest itself of broad responsibilities, it would seem appropriate to suggest that the Black Church begin to reflect on the approach that it has heroically assumed, shouldering the burden of being a spiritual refuge with social consciousness which has, at times and places, been more pronounced than at others. While this unevenness exasperates those who have a one-dimensional perspective of the Black Church, its genius is that it recognizes human beings as both spirit and body with a duality of needs which must be addressed, as both are constantly at risk in American society. Lincoln and Mamiya agree, stating:

> effective mission is the ability to determine where emphasis should be placed in light of existing realities. Contemporary needs are both deeply spiritual and agonizingly physical, and the resultant burden of the Black Church has never been more critical or more challenging.[23]

How does the Black Church continue to apply a social gospel that provided hope through slavery, sounded the trumpet of equality during the struggle for civil rights, and liberated the minds and spirits of its adherents? In an era where the Black population possesses its highest accumulation of wealth (which is still significantly lower than Whites), how does the church bridge capitalism with Christianity? How does the Black Church address social challenges such as health care, public education and unemployment, without abandoning its distinct and divine missionary mandate? And can the Black Church regain its historical place as a significant institution with the collective power to effect change?

Power Dynamics

> People in a revolution don't become part of the system; they destroy the system . . . The Negro revolution is no revolution because it condemns the system and then asks the system it has condemned to accept them.
>
> MALCOLM X

---

23. Lincoln and Mamiya, *The Black Church in the African American Experience*, 397.

James Cone argues that power offers the authority for a person to determine his or her own position in relationships in society.[24] It was through this lens that Europeans came to understand the enslavement of Africans as an extension or fulfillment of biblical mandate and continued to reap the social and economic benefits of the slave trade. In his opening paragraph, H. Richard Niebuhr makes a case for the church's corruption by power:

> In dealing with such major social evils as war, slavery, and social inequality, it has discovered convenient ambiguities in the letter of the Gospels which enabled it to violate their spirit and to ally itself with the prestige and power those evils had gained . . .[25]

Niebuhr's point was that the church itself can use, and in fact had used, the Bible to not only justify atrocities, but place itself in a social position of power as well—power to inform, invalidate and enforce. This social power positioning of the Christian church at times was used to serve the purposes of White social dominance,[26] blurring the line between spiritual mission and social function. Thus, religion came to be a mechanism of social control that also dictated the reality of those being oppressed:

> [T]he life of the slaveholder and others of that culture was that of extending white inhumanity to excruciating limits, involving the enslavement of Africans and the annihilation of Indians [sic]. The life of the slave was the slave ship, the auction block, and the plantation regime. It involved the attempt to define oneself without the ordinary historical possibilities of self-affirmation. Therefore when the master and slave spoke of God, they could not possibly be referring to the same reality.[27]

The larger implication of this situation is that the conditional lack of power created contextual competition for its attainment, and, as individuals began to satisfy their need for personal, Westernized manifestations of social promotion, the power separation and distinction became more pronounced—fostering feelings of confusion, conflict, and contempt. An historical example of this being Bacon's Rebellion, where a White property owner in Jamestown, Virginia developed plans to seize Native American lands in an effort to acquire more property for himself and others while

---

24. Cone, *Black Theology and Black Power*.
25. Niebuhr, *The Social Sources of Denominationalism*, 3.
26. Loewen, *Lies My Teacher Told Me*.
27. Cone, *God of the Oppressed*, 10.

nullifying the threat of Indian raids. When refused militia support by Virginia's elite, Bacon condemned the oppressive practices of the rich and led an attack on their homes and property that inspired an alliance of White and Black bond laborers, as well as slaves. To protect their position of power, the elite planters shifted their reliance on indentured English-speaking servants in favor of importing more Black slaves. In addition, they extended special privileges to poor Whites: White settlers received greater access to Native American lands, White servants were allowed to police slaves through patrols and militias, and measures were taken to avoid competition between free and slave labor. According to Michelle Alexander, "these measures effectively eliminated the risk of future alliances between black slaves and poor whites."[28] Poor Whites suddenly had a direct, personal stake in the existence of a structuralized power dynamic and responded to the logic of their situation by seeking ways to expand their privileged position.[29]

Europeans found biblical and ideological justification for their imperialistic practices. The concept of the Great Commission was a religious belief held since the Puritan period that the United States had a providential mission to tame and Christianize the land, and, the doctrine of Manifest Destiny reflected an ideology that the United States was destined to control the continent from the Atlantic to the Pacific. The creation and maintenance of inequality, through imperial practices, was based on domination and subordination, which we see, from the outset, created an extraordinarily inequitable power dynamic—those with power increased in social standing, and those without were increasingly subject to the powerful's ideals and practices. While the valiant efforts to end oppression and achieve greater levels of equality have brought about significant changes in the overt, legalized, and sanctioned practices of the United States, "these new rules have been justified by new rhetoric, new language, and new social consensus, while producing many of the same results"[30]—a "preservation through transformation" power dynamic where White privilege is maintained, though the rules and rhetoric change.[31] Making sense of this dynamic requires that we pay close attention to the systems and structures that resulted and the culture that was created.

---

28. Alexander, *The New Jim Crow*, 25.
29. Morgan, *American Slavery, American Freedom*.
30. Alexander, *The New Jim Crow*, 21.
31. Siegel, "Why Equal Protection No Longer Protects," 1111.

Social Structure

To make strides toward establishing a new framework, we must begin with the frank acknowledgement that White America has been historically "weak-willed in ensuring justice" and has continued to resist the full acceptance of those with less power.[32] This creates a social structure that has persistent, ordered, and patterned inequity among individual and institutional arrangements, specifically the systematic distribution of power and access to resources possessed by individuals and communities. This structure entails barriers and constraints that are more burdensome for those with the least amount of power and fewest accesses to resources, leading to "meaning-systems" that, "while originally only ideas, gain force as they are reproduced in the material conditions of society."[33] The power inequity stems from the actions of individuals and institutions that have adopted systemic and structural social practices, which with the resulting material conditions become a part of and reinforcement for contingent applications and meanings.

Reviewing the Constitution, it is clear that the intent and content was largely based on a power dynamic with social, economic and political implications, affording rights to Whites as a means of creating distance from and competition within certain, perceived, inferior groups. These statutes both ideologically supported the dominant narrative of power and also fostered and furthered the inequities that gave systems and structures their stratifying force. Martin Luther King addressed this dynamic by saying,

> Negroes are almost instinctively cohesive. We band together readily, and against white hostility we have an intense and wholesome loyalty to each other. We are acutely conscious of the need, and sharply sensitive to the importance, of defending our own. Solidarity is a reality in Negro life, as it always has been among the oppressed. On the other hand, Negroes are capable of becoming competitive, carping and, in an expression of self-hate, suspicious and intolerant of each other. A glaring weakness in Negro life is lack of sufficient mutual confidence and trust.[34]

The lack of individual and institutional trust, along with limited access to resources, created a culture among Black churches and within the Black community counter to the one passed down from Black foremothers and

---

32. West, *Race Matters*, 7.
33. López, *White By Law*, 10.
34. Washington, ed., *A Testament of Hope*, 307.

forefathers that equipped Black folk "with cultural armor" to beat back the demons of hopelessness, meaninglessness, lovelessness and competitiveness.[35] This armor constituted ways of life and struggle, and consisted of cultural structures of meanings and feelings that created and sustained a sense of community.[36] Addressing what happened and how that changed begins with the recognition that culture within the Black community has changed and has been accompanied by a lack of adaptation by the Black Church.

Culture

Religion is a critical aspect of culture. Along with language, common folkways, mores, and a shared history, religion should be considered one of the building blocks of culture. Thus,

> culture is essentially a construct that describes the total body of belief, behaviors, knowledge, sanctions, values and goals that mark the way of life of a people . . . In the final analysis it comprises the things that people have, the things they do, and what they think.[37]

While the modern use of the term "culture" obscures the original, dynamic, and creative meaning of "tending, harvesting, or cultivating," retaining this active sense alerts us to the fact that culture is not some inert abstract reality, but is always in process, both in the sense that it is always affecting and always being actively produced.[38] Meaning, specific historical context, may inform culture, but different functionality influences it. Consequently, culture is not a monolithic stationary entity that should be rejected, accommodated, or even transformed as a whole, it is a dynamic process which should be interacted in a critical, discriminating, and constructive manner.[39]

So what is the implication for the Black Church? The internalization of a counter-culture that encourages and rewards accumulation, greed, and gain not only harms the individual, but hinders the sense of community as well—a critical component by which the historic Black Church and social gospel are understood. Acquiescing to a worldview predicated on an

---

35. West, *Race Matters*, 23.
36. Ibid.
37. Tanner, *Theories of Culture*, 27.
38. Guder, *Missional Church*, 151.
39. Ibid.

inequitable social structure directly places the Black community in the patterns of domination and subordination. And, in order for these patterns to be purged, the behavior must be identified and addressed as the tragic response of a people bereft of resources in confronting a power dynamic that results in lives of "random nows," characterized by fortuitous and fleeting moments preoccupied with "getting over," seeking to acquire pleasure, property, and power by any means necessary.[40] Under these circumstances, Black existential angst deriving from a lived experience inflicted by a White social structure that has permeated Black culture[41] cannot be understood solely in spiritual terms. On some level, the Black Church has to engage and address the social reality of what Kimberlé Crenshaw labels "the relationship of coercion and consent." She argues that Black people are boxed in largely because there is a consensus among many Whites that oppression is legitimate. This is where coercion and consent can be understood: ideology convinces one group that the coercive domination of another is legitimate, causing the dominated group to consent with the hope of someday being in a coercive position.[42]

As a culture-forming institution, the Black Church needs to rediscover its cultivating process, which produces Black people in a particular way—characterized by love and care for neighbor, taking into account the current social realities of the Black condition. Given that most Western Christian institutions have been birthed by the advantaged class, it is expected that they would minimize Jesus' gospel of liberation for the powerless by interpreting lack of resources or access as a spiritual condition unrelated to social, economic and political phenomena. The culture and structure of society's power dynamic have a stranglehold on the soul of the Black community, and until removed, the Black community will continue to suffer. In true prophetic fashion, Cornel West testifies, "any disease of the soul must be conquered by a turning of one's soul. This turning is done through one's own affirmation of one's worth—an affirmation fueled by the concern of others."[43] The first social gospel dimension for the Black Church to reclaim and recontextualize is the historical praxis of community, self-sacrifice, and speaking truth to power instead of the current social practice

---

40. West, *Race Matters*, 10–25.
41. Ibid., 27.
42. Crenshaw, "Race, Reform, and Retrenchment," 1331.
43. West, *Race Matters*, 29.

of individualism, self-interest, and pursuit of personal gain which has corrupted the soul of the Church and community.

The evangelical traditions of the past, which set the norm for the early Black Church, only required evidence of a sincere calling from God to enter the ministry. A second social gospel dimension for the Black Church to reclaim and recontextualize is the training of clergy. A prudent approach for the future would be to add *practical* education to address the inherent fractures of life in the Black community. It is to this second dimension that we now turn.

Leadership Education & Training

A wise man will hear and increase learning,
And a man of understanding will attain wise counsel . . .

PROVERBS 1:5

A look at the history of Christianity in the context of slavery also reveals various perspectives in which to view leadership education and training. Gayraud Wilmore contends that the first religious leaders recognized by slaves were not appointed out of their number by White missionaries, "but those men and women who had either learned their priestcraft in Africa, or were taught by someone else who had."[44] He furthers that the inept practice of native religion (inept because it did not produce desired results) resulted in

> the taking on of more and more of the language, ritual trappings, and symbolization of Christianity until the old African religions were overpowered and the first Christian exhorters began to emerge as confidants and assistants of the itinerant white preachers.[45]

By the eve of the Civil War, the vast majority of slaves were American-born, and the cultural and linguistic barriers which had impeded the evangelization and conversion of earlier generations of African-born slaves were no longer a problem.[46]

---

44. Wilmore, *Black Religion and Black Radicalism*, 49.
45. Ibid.
46. Raboteau, *Slave Religion*, 212.

Preachers licensed by the church and hired by the master were supplemented by "slave preachers" licensed only by the spirit. The "slave preachers" became characterized by how well they told the story. Prohibited from reading, their knowledge of word structure carried less value than the feeling they could inspire, and the feeling was tied directly to how well they merged biblical stories with concrete images of the slaves' social situation. This pattern continues in today's contemporary context, as "Black churches usually do not emphasize academic degrees as a criterion for preaching, because they do not associate a learned discourse with storytelling."[47] Indeed, on some level, many Blacks are suspicious of academically-credentialed ministers in the pulpit because of their identification with the perpetuation of the White, slavemaster's Christian gospel that kept Blacks in physical and psychological bondage. For many in the Black community, one does not need formal education in order to tell God's story, and this has created a perspective rift based on the necessity, value, and contextual significance of formal education as it relates to Black pastoral leadership.

Much of the debate about education finds its roots in the story of the slave preacher: were slave preachers an instrument for accommodation to the status quo or a vessel to exercise slave autonomy? On the one hand, slave preachers were criticized as being the "mouthpieces of the masters," on the other, the freedom messages given and insurrections led by slave preachers are well-documented. Likewise, the dualities regarding education exist: does it perpetuate dominant social structure ideals or assist in liberation from encountered social realities? A serious response to this question requires inquiry into the development of class stratification within the Black community, a sociocultural phenomenon/reality that made its way into the Black Church.[48]

Class Stratification

According to Niebuhr, the division within the church has been caused more by "the direct and indirect operation of economic factors than by the influence of any other major interest of man." He was able to demonstrate that early church generations were usually comprised of those on the "lower economic and cultural scale" and that their church practices could be distinguished from other generations who had elevated up the economic

47. Cone, *God of the Oppressed*, 53.
48. West, *Race Matters*, 53.

scale.⁴⁹ This is to say that power helps to produce hierarchies; hierarchies in turn produce classism. What Niebuhr found was that the "organization which is loudest in its praise of brotherhood and most critical of race and class discriminations in other spheres is the most disunited group of all, nurturing in its own structure that same spirit of division which it condemns in other relations."⁵⁰ This is reflected biblically in the relationship between the Sadducees and Pharisees, as the rift between the two had more to do with class differences than with any major religious distinction.⁵¹

The civil rights movement permitted a large number of Blacks to benefit from the American economic boom of the sixties. The "American Dream" was presented principally in terms of access to, and accumulation of, resources. And, like any American group achieving contemporary middle-class station for the first time, Black entrée into the culture of *"access and accumulation"* made social status an obsession.⁵² Nowhere was this more clearly evident than in the Black Church, which began to splinter into different congregational types: ones that tended to reflect more an Africanized style of worship—equating "African" with "uncultured" and attended by those categorized as lower-class; and those that reflected more of Westernized style—equating Western with being "cultured" and preferred by most thought to be middle-class. This marked the Black community's gross deterioration of personal, familial, and communal relations, and in this way, the class stratification produced by integration has resulted in the community's internal turmoil and existential meaninglessness.⁵³

This caused Black churches to no longer identify with the Black underclass—following the money of the middle-class, instead of following the ministry of Jesus. So, as the culture of the Black community began to change, the ethos and expectation of the Black pastoral leader began to change as well. Distant from the vibrant tradition of resistance, vital communal understanding bonded by ethical ideals, and a credible sense of political struggle, Black Church leadership began to reveal the tame and genteel face

---

49. Niebuhr, *The Social Sources of Denominationalism*.

50. Ibid.

51. The Sadducees were viewed as aristocrats, many of whom belonged to, or were associated with, the priesthood (cf. Acts 5:17). In *Antiquities*, Josephus records, "They win over the wealthy. They do not have the people on their side." Contrarily, the Pharisees were viewed more as commoners because they didn't cut themselves off from society. See Stanton, *The Gospels and Jesus*, 258–62.

52. West, *Race Matters*, 55.

53. Ibid., 56.

of the Black middle-class and reflect the values of Black middle-class life: professional conscientiousness, personal accomplishment, and cautious adjustment.[54] This created a schism in the tending of community needs as there were, and are, two perceived communities—one that has assimilated, acculturated, and ascended; and one that has not. In an interview, Bishop John Hurst Adams addressed this:

> ... an issue I ought to lift up because it is a real concern to me, is the model of ministry to which our young clergy look upon ... the television preachers where they see big crowds and big money, both of which can have a corrupting influence. But the models of ministry I wrote about, for example, during the Civil Rights era were people who are cause oriented, and justice oriented. The models of ministry which our young clergy look to now are the success images of money and people, big crowds, and big money. And that's an issue which I think bears some responsibility ...[55]

How can there be synergy and solidarity within the Black Church and community when the cultural cohesion has changed so drastically?

The Reconciliatory Role of Education

In a recent CNN investigation, thirty-two percent of Black middle-class households met the education threshold for economic security, meaning that at least one member of the household has a bachelor's degree.[56] In contrast, the Interdenominational Theological Center in Atlanta, a consortium of six Black seminaries, has estimated that only ten to twenty percent of the Black clergy nationwide have completed their professional education.[57] The obvious dichotomy, as noted by Lincoln and Mamiya, is that the educational level of the Black middle-class has already surpassed that of the majority of this country's Black clergy. This is critical because it sets the stage for an institution with a low number of seminary-trained clergy for whom the tradition of being *called* is most important, attempting to pastor an increasing number of educated middle-class Blacks whose culture prefers *credentials*. This has led to alienation from the Black Church

---

54. Ibid.

55. Interview with Bishop John Hurst Adams, ICAM Ford Ethics Project.

56. Taken from CNN's *Black in America* initiative which expanded into the investigation series, "State of Black America."

57. Lincoln and Mamiya, *The Black Church in the African American Experience.*

The Future Horizon for a Prophetic Tradition

in a historic sense, where traditional preaching styles, worship practices, and ecclesial formulas designed to elicit feeling no longer have an impact. Their expectation of more probing sermons, intellectual stimulation, and spiritual nurturing that points in a non-demonstrative, non-emotive manner is the challenge facing current and future pastoral leaders.

In 1990, a study conducted by C. Eric Lincoln and Lawrence H. Mamiya, found the median age of all Black clergy to be 52 years old.[58] In a 2001 Pulpit and Pew survey, the median age for Black pastors was 53. Table 7.1[59] shows the percentage of Black and White clergy in various age groups. We see that 61% of all Black clergy are 51 years of age or older, while 50% of White clergy are in that category. Black clergy who are 50 years of age or less constitute 39% of the sample.

Age Group	Black %	White %
Less than 45	12%	30%
45 to 50	27%	20%
51 to 60	31%	31%
61 +	30%	19%

Table 7.1. Age of Black and White Clergy

I highlight the age factor to bring attention to education level's compounding effect on the Black Church. With the majority of its pastors over the age of 50, with little to no seminary training, the Black Church is far from meeting the increasing education level of the community. Studies have shown that community outreach programs of Black churches, working with government and foundation funds, and working on gender advancement issues are highly correlated with the level of clergy education.[60] So what opportunity does this present for the Black Church?

Like Lincoln and Mamiya, I recognize that formal seminary education is not a panacea for all the ills of the Black Church, or for the Black community. But, it is my contention that a *practical* education that combines the foundations of a formalized curriculum with a focus on the Black experience and public policy, would not only benefit Black clergy, but the entire Christian

---

58. See ibid.

59. Becky R. McMillan, National Survey Results—By Race, Pulpit and Pew Research on Pastoral Leadership, 2003.

60. Lincoln and Mamiya, *The Black Church in the African American Experience*, 130.

community and civil society as a whole. Though not seminary approved, there is a wealth of pastoral knowledge within the Black community. Education presents a reconciling opportunity that brings together the breadth and depth of learned experience represented by Black pastors, and the training and endorsement possessed by seminary institutions. Unfortunately, according to Cone, White seminarians, and some Blacks as well, have convinced themselves that only White foundations provide the accepted and approved construct for theological reflection. He continues,

> they do not recognize the narrowness of their experience and the particularity of their theological expressions. They like to think of themselves as *universal* people. That is why most seminaries emphasize the need for appropriate tools in doing theology, which always means *white* tools, i.e., knowledge of the language and thought of white people. They fail to recognize that other people also have thought[s] about God and have something significant to say about Jesus' presence in the world.[61]

A *practical* education could help enhance the skills and effectiveness of Black clergy by fusing the areas of spiritual nurturing, theological understanding, and biblical interpretation, with accounting, financial management, economic development, capacity building, and public policy to create a comprehensive learning context. As workplace specialization increases, the ministry remains one of the few particular areas for generalists—as one interviewee quipped, "The Black pastor is expected to know a little something about everything." Black Church clergy represent "those much needed people who attempt to relate to the whole spectrum of human needs in the interests of a broader and deeper humanity"[62] and a practical education that appreciates and understands the ideological roots and illuminates the content of White scholarship through that paradigm would be advantageous.

While I believe that the Black pastor should be familiar with the various civic spheres affecting their members and the community, I must note that I am not a proponent of the Black pastor shouldering the burden to be and do everything. Older pastors can serve as mentors, as the Black Church tradition is blessed with a variety of extraordinary leaders who are approaching the end of fruitful careers, and become resources for the next generation of public theologians and clergy in a constructive manner that encourages

---

61. Cone, *God of the Oppressed*, 14.
62. Lincoln and Mamiya, *The Black Church in the African American Experience*, 400.

cooperation, collaboration, and building of partnerships.[63] A glaring omission in the Black Church tradition, and Black liberation theology for that matter, is a public policy agenda. The challenge for the future is whether Black clergy will become well-versed enough to transcend their institutional boundaries so that they may access resources to become effective in this arena. It is to this fourth area that we now shift.

Partnerships

> If I have a choice between a Christian whose heart isn't in the right place,
> and an atheist who is willing to help and further my cause,
> give me the atheist every time.
>
> MICHAEL ERIC DYSON

Equality, as understood within the Black Church tradition, is both problematic and redemptive.[64] It is problematic because its historical connotation and pursuit implied that once equal rights were achieved, the ills of the Black condition would be solved. It is redemptive because Black Churches have dealt with the problematic in ways that have also addressed the underlying practice of equity, which makes social transformation possible and stands as the foundational principle in American democratic idealism—*access*.[65] The practice of equity has been the glaring omission within institutions, systems and structures that have historically dehumanized, disenfranchised, and destabilized Blacks. But, Black congregations are well-positioned and have extraordinary potential to transform and enhance the condition of the Black

---

63. Franklin, *Crisis in the Village*, 135.

64. See the definition of "the Black Christian tradition" in Paris, *The Social Teaching of the Black Churches*. Paris claims that "the moral and political significance of the black churches is derived from a common source of authority, the black Christian tradition. Here the thought and practice of religion, politics, and morality are integrally related. That is to say, the one always implies the other. Whenever religion, politics, and morality are isolated from one another, the tradition itself is severely threatened" (12). This critical principle, according to Paris, is fundamental for "justifying and motivating all endeavors by blacks for survival and social transformation."

65. This is an argument voiced by Walter Earl Fluker who believes that three underlying practices exist—recognition, respectability, and loyalty. Fluker, "Recognition, Respectability, and Loyalty," in Smith, *New Day Begun*, 114.

community in both the personal and public spheres. With this in mind, given the ironic, even paradoxical manner in which Black churches have continued to maintain loyalty to a system that has historically abused their commitment, I am suggesting a reclaiming and recontextualizing of a fourth social gospel dimension—institutional partnerships.

In September 1967, the National Council of Churches Division of Christian Life and Work sponsored a national conference on the urban crisis in America. Held in Washington, D.C., it brought together Black and White church activists and race relations executives. The Black delegates, many of whom were members of the National Committee of Negro Churchmen, insisted in the opening session that the conference be divided into two caucuses, one Black and the other White. They further proposed that the caucuses meet separately for most of the time and come together for a final plenary session. The motion to divide the conference was sustained and the two groups convened to discuss the nature and feasibility of interracial alliances. In a drafted statement for the final session, the White caucus condemned the practices of the White church and, in an unprecedented display of maturity, unequivocally affirmed the position of Blacks and called upon Whites to stop trying to dominate liberal coalitions with Blacks.[66] According to Gayraud Wilmore, the Washington conference "was a dramatic demonstration of the influence of the black power movement within the precincts of the American religious establishment" and it "inaugurated an era of confrontation and negotiation between blacks and whites unprecedented in twentieth-century American Christianity."[67]

The statement produced at the Washington conference highlights two points: 1) when the Black community is relatively integrated with White society, the elements of the Black community tend to recede from the interaction while the White elements come to the fore; and 2) the contribution of the Black community is no longer community-credible because it has been manipulated in ways that render it no longer community-reflective. Undergirding these points, or better even, practices, is what Robert Putnam terms *social capital*:

> Connections among individuals—social networks and the norms of reciprocity and trustworthiness that arise from them. Moreover, social capital is related to civic virtue in that the latter is "most

---

66. Wilmore and Cone, "The Church and the Urban Crisis, Statements from Black and White Caucuses," 43–47.

67. Wilmore, *Black Religion and Black Radicalism*, 230.

powerful when it is embedded in a dense network of reciprocal social relations. A society of many virtuous, but isolated individuals is not necessarily rich in social capital."[68]

According to Walter Earl Fluker, this description of social capital and its role in creating and sustaining community is important in two ways: 1) social capital provides networks and alliances for civic engagement that can be inclusive and beneficial; and 2) social capital derives its life and power from the reciprocal norms that it engenders and sustains.[69]

Strategic Alliances

Martin Luther King called the art of alliances complex and intricate.[70] You could make the argument that his assertion was accurate because building alliances is much more involved than than the isolated practice of sermon preparation. It entails an acknowledgement of self and common interests, validation of single and shared identity, and affirmation of individual and collective resources. If, as King argued, we employ the principle of selectivity along these lines, we will find millions of allies who, in serving themselves, also support the Black Church and Black community, "and on such sound foundations unity and mutual trust and tangible accomplishment will flourish."[71]

Another social reality that is advantageous to examine is who has the power to assign, limit, or amend alliance construction. When Cornel West speaks of perpetrators of free-market fundamentalism and authoritarianism, he defines them as "plutocratic leaders, corporate elites, elected officials, [and] arrogant authoritarians."[72] In other words, those in socially-constructed positions who have the ability and authority, based on access, to designate the parameters of association. In the realm of the Black Church, such persons would be the pastors, ministers and any other "gate-keeper" within the congregation; while in larger civil society, they would be CEOs, executive directors and any person assigned to manage a project. This is significant because in order for an alliance to be truly authentic, each party

68. Putnam, *Bowling Alone*, 19.
69. Fluker, "Recognition, Respectability, and Loyalty," 117.
70. Washington, *A Testament of Hope*, 309.
71. Ibid., 310.
72. West, *Democracy Matters*, 21–23.

must recognize and respect the position and resources possessed by the other. The simple fact is that there cannot be authentic alliances without serious commitment to honesty, sensitivity and transparency—and not the principles of mendacity, manipulation, and misinformation.[73] Don Williams, Chairman of the Trammell Crow Company, recounts the following:

> When I began this [community empowerment] work, I assumed that well-intentioned, well-connected business leaders like myself would be welcomed in the inner city. To the contrary, I found a deep—and often well deserved—distrust of outside institutions and their representatives, particularly businessmen. I heard stories about the many ways in which the business community misrepresented its intentions.[74]

Shared-Power

As they studied successful change efforts, Barbara Crosby and John Bryson "realized that organizations had to find a way to tap each other's resources (broadly conceived) in order to work effectively on public problems. That is, they had to engage in sharing activities, which vary in level of commitment and loss of autonomy."[75] This brings to bear a critical point: most leaders are either unwilling or uncomfortable forfeiting autonomy and/or power—this is especially true in the Black Church, an observation made earlier. In order for this theory to become praxis, the philosophical perspective has to change to visualize what can be accomplished by a shared-power structure that otherwise is less effective, impactful, and extensive. Social critics highlight the division between those who have access and those who do not as the relevant factor in the giving and silencing of voices[76]—shared-power arrangements may be most useful in reminding those with little *formal* authority how powerful they can be through collaboration, "and in reminding those in a supposedly powerful position just how much they rely on numerous stakeholders for any *real* power they have."[77]

---

73. Ibid., 28.
74. Humphries, *In the City for Good*, 99.
75. Crosby and Bryson, *Leadership for the Common Good*, 17.
76. Smith and Seltzer, *Race, Class, and Culture*, 133–38.
77. Crosby and Bryson, *Leadership for the Common Good*, 29.

The Future Horizon for a Prophetic Tradition

For instance, given that only 6.4% of congregations worship with over 500 participants,[78] shared-power arrangements could enhance collective group power by reducing the individual risk for participants and sharing responsibility—no one entity gets all the credit (a tough pill to swallow for some Black leaders!), no one entity shoulders all the blame. Smaller Black congregations that have little financial resources and minimal infrastructure, but bring the energy of active citizens who can supply first-hand knowledge of community needs, can partner with larger megachurches that have financial resources and institutional capacity. A major critique of megachurches is their isolationism from the local community. As one executive director noted,

> They [megachurches] feel that they have enough power as a church and community and that they don't need to participate with or tie into a community organization . . .[79]

Martin Luther King stated, "action is not in itself a virtue; its goals and its forms determine its value."[80] History has shown that individual and collective power must be harnessed and forcefully wielded if it expects to overcome systemic and structural power. From women not attaining the right to vote until 1920, indigenous people until 1924 and Blacks until 1964, the glaring omission from the initial efforts of each was their inability to generate organized, collective democratic pressure. Yet, as a marshaled collaborative force that critically-engaged the wealthy, White-male dominated power structure, their goal of voting rights was achieved. This type of democratic work opportunity offered by shared-power arrangement is championed by political philosophers and organizational theorists such as Mary Dietz, whose interest in revitalized citizenship entailed collective and participatory engagement; Ronald Heifetz, who argued that a relinquishing of autonomous power contributes to group goal attainment; Jim Collins, who articulated the significance of ambition first and foremost for macro over micro success; and Sharon Dalon Parks, who specifically writes:

> Our culture tells us we are autonomous. Actually, we are each an integral part of multiple systems. The challenge is to reflect critically on our reality, learn to see the patterns, and recognize how context driven people are, that is how much people are shaped by

---

78. Taken from Hartford Institute for Religion Research Report, 2010.
79. Mamiya, "River of Struggle, River of Freedom."
80. Washington, *A Testament of Hope*, 179.

the expectations of their social milieu . . . Within a systemic, holistic view, one has to give up the good self for the complicit self—-an integral, responsible part of the fabric of the wider commons for both good and ill.[81]

---

81. Parks, *Leadership Can Be Taught*, 54–56.

Chapter Five

Conclusion

Introduction

BASED ON THE HISTORY and perspectival changes recounted in previous chapters, it is clearly evident that a different approach to mission and leadership would be required to remedy the acculturation, stratification, and disconnection of the Black Church. Such an approach would have to overcome the loss of historical identity characterized by the lack of relationality between church and community. It would have to encompass not only an intentional level of theological reflection upon mission, but a focused perspective on practical, preparatory theological education for pastoral leadership as well. The approach would have to embrace a Black cultural understanding and heritage of "community" as an augmentation rather than an impediment. And, while addressing community crises and developments, it would have to avoid the social, economic, and political trap of compromise and cooptation. These needs point toward an opportunity to renew the Black Church's prophetic engagement through a process of missional and leadership transformation—a development with wider implications for the future.

The Cultural Dimension

As farm and plantation slaves, then as domestic servants in White households, Blacks witnessed the most intimate aspects of White life and culture, but very few Whites knew anything about Black people or their culture. In fact, some scholars have viewed aspects of Black cultural creations as aberrational attempts to mimic mainstream White culture,[1] while other scholars have claimed that Blacks are simply American and, having been 'Americanized,' possess no values or culture to guard and protect.[2] Such arguments refrain from giving Blacks the minimum presuppositions granted to other hyphenated American populations, "which is to say that their origins were elsewhere and that coming from elsewhere, if they have a viable history, they must also have an effective culture."[3] This refrain refuses to recognize that all persons come from, and live within particular contexts, and therefore, "possess specific cultural perspectives that are historically conditioned and shape the way they understand, see, and experience life."[4]

Culture is the form of religion and religion is the heart of culture. Paul Tillich's insight about the relationship between religion and culture is important in a discussion about the Black Church.[5] Religion is expressed in cultural forms like music and song, prayer and preaching, and modes of worship, to provide a few examples. But, religion is also the heart of culture because it raises the core values of that culture to ultimate levels, giving them legitimacy. The core values of Black culture like liberation, justice, equality, and equity on all levels are raised to ultimate heights and legitimated in the Black Church, and, on many occasion, were given birth and nurtured in its womb. According to Newbigin, culture is human behavior in corporate aspect—where the Black cultural heritage was vibrant and alive, so was the Black religious tradition, as much of Black culture was forged in the heart of Black religion and the Black Church.[6] A demise of the Black Church would have profound implications for the preservation of Black culture.

---

1. Examples of this view are found in the works of E. Franklin Frazier and Gunnar Myrdal.

2. Glazer and Moynihan, *Beyond the Melting Pot*.

3. Lincoln and Mamiya, *The Black Church in the African American Experience*, 3.

4. Guder, *Missional Church*, 40.

5. Tillich's theology of culture involved a dialectical relationship between religion and culture. His broad definition of religion as "ultimate concern" or "ultimate value" makes it possible to see how religion sacralizes the central values of a culture or a group of people. In his view of Christianity however, Tillich also provided for the possibility of religion transcending culture and offering a critique of it in his notion of the "protestant principle." Adams, *Paul Tillich's Philosophy of Culture, Science, and Religion*.

6. Newbigin, *The Gospel in a Pluralistic Society*, 188.

THE FUTURE HORIZON FOR A PROPHETIC TRADITION

The Black Church as Central Mediating Structure

Common in the American understanding of Black subculture is the assumption that the Black Church constituted the central institutional sector in Black communities. Reliable investigators such as Du Bois, Woodson, Frazier, Raboteau, Lincoln and Mamiya have consistently underscored the fact that the Black Church was one of the few stable and coherent institutions to emerge from slavery.[7] Among quasi-free Blacks, mutual aid societies and churches stood as the first institutions created by Black people. For example, the Free African Society, a mutual aid society founded by Richard Allen and Absalom Jones in 1787, gave birth to Mother Bethel A.M.E. Church in 1794.[8] During Reconstruction, according to Lincoln and Mamiya, the pattern for their central and dominant institutional role was established when churches became "the centers of the numerous Black communities in the South" that were formed as former slaves but separated from the plantation base to which they previously belonged.[9] Not only did the Black Church give birth to new institutions such as schools, lending institutions, insurance companies, and low-income housing, it provided multifarious levels of community involvement such as an academy and arena for political activities, in addition to the traditional concerns of worship, moral fabric, and social standing.

Some of the more astute visionary church leaders such as Adam Clayton Powell (Harlem, New York), Joseph Lowry (Mobile, Alabama), Ralph Abernathy (Montgomery, Alabama), and C.K. Steele (Tallahassee, Florida), saw the need to develop secular relationships in order to cope with more complex, integrated issues facing the Black community. However, an expanded approach did not require a distinction in focus of the Black Church. The resultant interplay and interaction allowed clergy and church members to influence the systems and structures of the larger society. King speaks of this in terms of "alliance politics," where deep structural changes can be achieved by a broad coalition of organizations representing a variety of interests, "based upon some self-interest of each component group and a common interest into which they merge."[10] This view challenges contempo-

---

7. DuBois, *The Negro Church*; Woodson, *The History of the Negro Church*; Frazier, *The Negro Church in America*; Raboteau, *Slave Religion*; Lincoln and Mamiya, *The Black Church in the African American Experience*.

8. Mitchell, *Black Church Beginnings*, 66.

9. Lincoln and Mamiya, *The Black Church in the African American Experience*, 8.

10. King, Jr., *Where Do We Go From Here: Chaos or Community?*

rary Black churches to enhance their activities and power by accessing all of its potential resources from inside and outside the traditional ecclesiastical framework. In contrast, most views of religion, based on the rhetoric of separation of church and state, "assume a posture of complete differentiation, where the spheres of the polity and the economy are completely separated from religion, do not intersect, and have very little interaction."[11] My contention is that such a view, when applied to the Black Church, distorts its mediating significance and confuses its civic-minded nature.

The Black Church Tradition as Civic-Minded

Although it has been variously expressed in both religious symbols and political concepts, the Black Church's appropriation of the Christian faith is grounded in the principle of God's involvement in humanity and humanity's participation with God. In brief, the life and the mission of the Black Church have been fundamentally rooted in the sovereignty and activity of God relative to the social condition of His people. From this standpoint, civic-minded encompasses more than engagement on behalf of a constituency, it also includes community and capacity building, or as Paris states, a politics that builds structures for human associations.[12] So, while the origins of Black Church civic engagement focused on the immediate conditional realities, the progression of civic engagement maintained a critical posture interrogating the larger systemic and structural causes.

The civic engagement of the Black Church offers two lessons on the relationship between religion and politics. First, it illustrates the potent point that American electoral politics depend upon the role of voluntary associations, and in the Black community, the Black Church is the dominant voluntary association. Second, as Paris highlights, politics is often too narrowly defined as "electoral," restricting the inclusion of the kind of community organizing and empowering activities which constitute the usual form of Black Church politics—food shelves, housing programs, and tending to the physical, emotional, and spiritual needs of the people. All of which, ultimately, are means of civic engagement as measurable civic power grows out of organized and mobilized people whose dignity and status have been acknowledged and affirmed.[13]

11. Lincoln and Mamiya, *The Black Church in the African American Experience*, 9–10.
12. Paris, *Black Leaders in Conflict*.
13. Paris, *The Social Teaching of the Black Churches*, 110–17.

Due to their social location and independent existence, Black churches often formed a potent civic base, particularly larger congregations. With a civic understanding and political meaning, Black voices, votes, and activity began to extend beyond the physical confines of the church and into the lived realities of their community. Lincoln and Mamiya believe that "because their voices and votes counted in the universe of black activity, the black churches were able to enlist the deepest loyalties of their constituents."[14] In all of the micro-varieties of Black civic engagement that have unfolded over several hundred years, the target has always been the macro-system of oppression that has often attempted and succeeded in defining the limits and choices of the Black subculture.[15] It is in relationship to this history and progression of oppression that the civic-minded nature of the Black Church must be seen.

Who Says?

There have been many important contributions made in an attempt to define the "Black Church," like those of James Cone, J. Deotis Roberts, C. Eric Lincoln, and Lawrence M. Mamiya, just to name a few. All sought to identify the distinct Black experience, and yet clarify the White mainstream conditions that colored the experience. In doing so, they furnished an understanding of how the liberating message of Jesus Christ functioned to empower Blacks, create a distinct community, and call for a different style of leadership and civic relationship. In many ways, each contribution targeted God's transformative work in the lives of Blacks and the possibilities for society as a whole. I have attempted here to demonstrate how and why this mixed-methods research is a work of public theology. Just as Cone, Roberts, Lincoln, and others have done, this endeavor sought to help the Black Church move forward drawing from a multitude of voices along the way, describing discussions, identifying challenges, and outlining suggestions. Theological and theoretical reflections were placed in conversation, and historical and practical insights integrated in an attempt to create a new horizon for the Black Church—one

---

14. Lincoln and Mamiya, *The Black Church in the African American Experience*, 207.

15. Genovese has also argued in *Roll, Jordan, Roll* that Black political choices during slavery were limited by the White system of domination. Such a view corresponds to my emphasis on the historical and contemporary mediating significance of the Black Church in relationship to other institutional spheres of society.

that connects the heritage and legacy of the past with the needs and hopes for the future.

With the rise of social sciences and other social disciplines in the past two decades, the creation and normative description of the "Black Church" took place. Most Black interpreters, trained in or familiar with social sciences, outlined and defined the theoretical and practical boundaries of the Black Church. These interpreters sought a unified Black church, or at the very least, cooperation among Black churches to address the social, economic and political problems of Black oppression.[16] Of note, the early constructive discourse of W.E.B. Du Bois regarding "the Negro Church" while descriptive and prescriptive, also articulated "a particular conception of what black churches ought to do in light of the depressing situation of blacks in the south at the end of the nineteenth century."[17] Although centrally responsible for the creation of "the Negro Church," Du Bois' work in comparison with other Black interpreters indicates a struggle to articulate "older notions of a unique spirituality alongside the new social scientific notion of 'the Black Church' as the principal social institution in Black life."[18] Hence the need to recontextualize the Black Church which was, and should be, more than "simply an organism for the propagation of religion."[19]

Mediating Accessibility

As Martin Kilson has observed, much of the interaction between the Black Church and civil society was characterized by "patron-client relationships" between urban machines and Black leaders. This interaction worked through "a small group of blacks who fashioned personalized links with influential whites, becoming clients of the whites for a variety of socio-political purposes."[20] The Black Church and community would be better served by more vested relationships that allow institutional and systemic access on a wider scale. Given its limited systemic and structural access, the Black community relies mightily on the Black Church, to be either an end,

16. Evans, *The Burden of Black Religion*, 8.
17. Ibid.
18. Ibid., 141.
19. Green and Driver, *W.E.B. Du Bois*, 228.
20. Kilson also points out that the exclusionary systemic practice of treating the Black community as an accessible resource rather than partner undermined Black development. Kilson, "Political Change in the Negro Ghetto, 1900–1940s."

The Future Horizon for a Prophetic Tradition

or no less than a means to an end. Religious institutions within the Black community are important resources for Black mobilization and participation. An extensive study of volunteerism in the United States conducted by Sidney Verba and colleagues found that many individuals learn civic skills through their religious institutions. The research reported that while over two-thirds of individuals in the United States have learned civic and organizing skills in their workplace, about two-fifths practice such skills in nonpolitical spaces, and nearly one-third reported practicing such skills in their worship environments.[21] The study concludes that, for several reasons, Blacks derive more participatory benefit from their churches stemming from the higher likelihood of church membership, Protestant affiliation, and exposure to relevant stimuli at their place of worship compared to the general population.[22]

During an initial conversation, one minister, when asked to identify the difference between the Black Church in a historical and contemporary context articulated, "The pulpit and pew have become so selective that the Black Church has become very ineffective." As he continued to explain, the link between pulpit consciousness and pew cognizance became apparent. The idea of "selective" preaching, or "selective" service, according to this pastor, follows the self-interest models of American individualism and totally counteracts the mediating role that should be played by the Black Church.

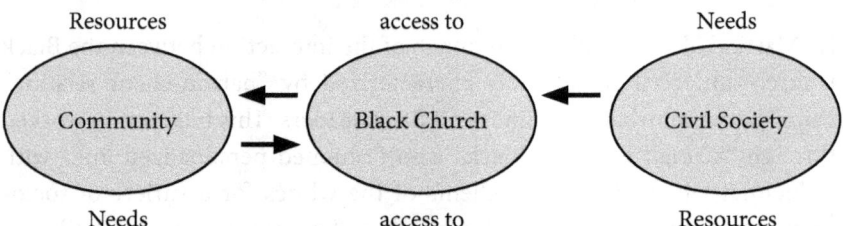

Figure 3.1. Connective Model of Community, Black Church, & Civil Society

Figure 3.1 illustrates the mediating position I hypothesize is held by the Black Church. The Black Church provides access to its constituency as needed by other civil society institutions, but provides no access for its constituency to those same institutions. As figure 3.1 shows, the Black Church has complete access to the resources and needs of the community, which directly foster its positioning as a pillar in and for the community.

21. Verba, et al., "Race, Ethnicity and Political Resources," 453–97.
22. Ibid.

Involvement of, as well as in, the church—a macro resource for civil society—nurtures skills that can be used in a larger context, so the presence of the Black Church might encourage political participation directly, or mobilize congregants and community members to challenge the practices of local, state, or federal agencies. Both direct political participation and mobilization emerge as a result of the Black Church's reciprocal relationship with, and commitment to, its community. Figure 3.1 also illustrates the potential reciprocal relationship between the Black Church and civil society. Church visits by political candidates, for instance, provide congregants with more knowledge of political affairs and candidates' agenda, but do nothing to include the community in strategic alliances.

As an indigenous institution that has survived everything from Reconstruction to a host of social and political movements throughout the late nineteenth and much of the twentieth century, the need for the Black Church to operate as a mediating resource for its community is critical. Its sustainability over time makes it the only Black institution which consistently promoted the affirmation and resistance of Blacks. This research assessed how the Black Church can heighten its presence given its communicative networks, capacity to promote institutional collaboration, and capability to provide essential resources.

Summary

Historically, according to Black Church scholar Aldon D. Morris, the institutions of the larger society were of little use to Blacks. Blacks were never equal partners in the institutions, systems and structures of a White-dominant society. In fact, they were intentionally excluded. As a result, the Black Church filled a large void by providing direction and support for activities such as civic engagement, clergy leadership, and a collective understanding of community causes.[23] The Black Church is unique "in that it was organized and developed by an oppressed group shut off from the institutional life of larger society."[24] It continues to function in that manner, though some have argued that larger institutional exclusion is not as expansive, pervasive, and oppressive.[25]

---

23. Morris, *The Origins of the Civil Rights Movement*, 4–5.
24. Ibid.
25. Pattillo-McCoy, *Black Picket Fences*.

The Future Horizon for a Prophetic Tradition

As remarked previously, indigenous culture and institutions of marginal groups are critical to the formation and legitimization of social movements, and the Black Church has functioned as both advocate and antagonist.[26]

This is a time for a dramatically new vision. King urged the Black Church and community "to turn more of their energies and focus creativity on the useful things that translate into power."[27] The current predicament of the Black Church requires more than a mere tinkering with long-assumed notions and traditionally-practiced methods about its identity and mission. The Black Church has been dislocated from its prior social role of champion of the community and carrier of culture, and it has lost its once privileged position of influence. So accommodated to a secular way of life, it is no longer obvious what justifies the Black Church's existence as a particular spiritual community.[28] This research has tried to identify phenomena in the Black Church as well as trends in broader society that have an impact on, and are impacted by, missional ecclesiology and pastoral leadership. The hope was to highlight implications and raise suggestions for the Black Church moving forward.

In the written Chinese language, the character signifying the idea of a "favorable opportunity" brings together characters that represent "good," "time," and "incipient moment."[29] Long-established traditions and long-standing practices have strongholds on any community, and the Black Church is no exception. Paradoxically, an institution that utilized the pews and pulpits to begin social movements has become lifeless and soulless because it is divorced from the reality of everyday Black life. Darrell Guder argues that these traditions and practices "constitute a way of seeing what the church is and what it is for . . . Such assumed patterns are brought into question, however, when the church recognizes that it has been demoted from its prior social importance and may have accommodated away something of its soul."[30] The call of the Black Church, in fact its commission, is to reclaim its soul, to take back the talking drums that were forcefully confiscated and have been willingly forfeited, in order to recontextualize the social gospel dimensions of its prophetic history. God's action involves

26. Marx, *Protest and Prejudice*, 94–98.
27. Washington, *A Testament of Hope*, 610–11.
28. Guder, *Missional Church*, 78.
29. Zeuschner, *Classical Ethics East and West*, 151–68.
30. Guder, *Missional Church*, 78.

CONCLUSION

a recognition of the growing ability of God's people to work towards their own liberation with God's guidance and grace. This favorable opportunity awaits the Black Church to once again provide the people with an imagination. *The community needs it; the world can use it.*

Bibliography

Adams, James Luther. *Paul Tillich's Philosophy of Culture, Science, and Religion*. New York: Harper & Row, 1965.
Ahlstrom, Sydney E. *A Religious History of the American People*. New Haven: Yale University Press, 1972.
Alexander, Michelle. *The New Jim Crow: Mass Incarceration in the Age of Colorblindness*. New York: The New, 2010.
Allen, Richard. *The Life Experiences and Gospel Labors of the Rt. Rev. Richard Allen*. Nashville: Abingdon, 1960.
Anderson, Claud. *Black Labor, White Wealth: The Search for Power and Economic Justice*. Edgewood: Duncan & Duncan, 1994.
Anderson, Victor. *Beyond Ontological Blackness*. New York: Continuum, 1995.
Andrews, Dale P. *Practical Theology for Black Churches: Bridging Black Theology and African American Folk Religion*. Louisville: Westminster John Knox, 2002.
Andrews, Marcellus. *The Political Economy of Hope and Fear: Capitalism and the Black Condition in America*. New York: New York University Press, 1999.
Anstey, Roger. *The Atlantic Slave Trade and British Abolition, 1760–1810*. London: MacMillan, 1975.
Aptheker, Herbert. *American Negro Slave Revolts*. New York: International, 1943.
———. *A Documentary History of the Negro People in the United States*. New York: Citadel, 1972.
Baer, Hans A. "Bibliography of Social Science Literature on Afro-American Religion in the United States." *Review of Religious Research* 29 (June 1988) 413–30.
Baer, Hans A., and Merrill Singer. *African-American Religion in the Twentieth Century*. Knoxville: The University of Tennessee Press, 1992.
Barth, Karl. *Church Dogmatics*. Translated by Thomas F. Torrance and Geoffrey W. Bromiley. New York: Scribner, 1936.
Battle, Michael. *The Black Church in America: African American Christian Spirituality*. Malden: Blackwell, 2006.
Bennett, Lerone Jr. *Before the Mayflower: A History of the Negro in America*. Baltimore: Penguin, 1966.
Bevans, Stephan B. *Models of Contextual Theology*. Maryknoll: Orbis, 2004.

BIBLIOGRAPHY

Bevans, Stephan B., and Roger P. Schroeder. *Constants in Context: A Theology of Mission for Today.* Maryknoll: Orbis, 2004.

Billings, R.A. "The Negro and His Church: A Psychogenetic Study." *Psychoanalytic Review* 21 (1934) 425–41.

Billingsley, Andrew. *Mighty Like a River: The Black Church and Social Reform.* New York: Oxford University Press, 1999.

Blackwell, James E. *The Black Community: Diversity and Unity.* New York: Harper & Row, 1975.

Boff, Leonardo. *Trinity and Society.* Eugene: Wipf & Stock, 1988.

Bosch, David J. *Transforming Mission: Paradigm Shifts in Theology of Mission.* Maryknoll: Orbis, 1991.

Bottomore, T.B., ed. and trans. *Karl Marx: Early Writings.* New York: McGraw-Hill, 1963.

Brown, Delwin, Sheila Greeve Davaney, and Kathryn Tanner, eds. *Converging On Culture: Theologians in Dialogue with Cultural Analysis and Criticism.* New York: Oxford University Press, 2001.

Brueggemann, Walter. *The Prophetic Imagination.* Philadelphia: Fortress, 1978.

Bunch, Ralph J. *The Political Status of the Negro in the Age of FDR.* Edited by Dewey W. Grantham. Chicago: University of Chicago Press, 1973.

Carter, Stephen L. *The Culture of Disbelief: How American Law and Politics Trivialize Religious Devotion.* New York: Basic, 1993.

Cauthen, Kenneth. *The Ethics of Belief: A Bio-Historical Approach.* Lima: CSS, 2001.

Chenu, Bruno. *The Trouble I've Seen.* Valley Forge: Judson, 2003.

Childs, James M., Jr. *Preaching Justice: The Ethical Vocation of Word and Sacrament Ministry.* Harrisburg: Trinity International, 2000.

Childs, John Brown. *The Political Black Minister: A Study in Afro-American Politics and Religion.* Boston: G.K. Hall, 1980.

Coalter, Milton J., John M. Mulder, and Louis B. Weeks, eds. *The Organizational Revolution: Presbyterians and American Denominationalism.* Louisville: Westminster John Knox, 1992.

Coleman, James. *Foundations of Social Theory.* Cambridge: Harvard University Press, 1990.

Collins, Jim. *Good to Great: Why Some Companies Make the Leap . . . and Others Don't.* New York: HarperCollins, 2001.

Cone, James. *Black Theology and Black Power.* New York: Seabury, 1975.

———. *A Black Theology of Liberation.* Maryknoll: Orbis, 1970.

———. *God of the Oppressed.* New York: Seabury, 1975.

Conley, Dalton. *Being Black, Living in the Red: Race, Wealth, and Social Policy in America.* Berkeley: University of California Press, 1999.

Conyers, James L., Jr. ed. *Black Cultures and Race Relations.* New York: Rowan & Littlefield, 2002.

Cooney, Patrick L., and Henry W. Powell. *The Life and Times of the Prophet Vernon Johns: The Father of the Civil Rights Movement.* Farmville: Vernon Johns Society, 1998.

Creswell, John W. *Qualitative Inquiry and Research Design: Choosing Among Five Traditions.* Thousand Oaks, CA: Sage, 1998.

Creswell John W., and Vicki L. Plano Clark. *Designing and Conducting Mixed Methods Research.* Thousand Oaks, CA: Sage, 2003.

Crosby, Barbara C., and John M. Bryson. *Leadership for the Common Good: Tackling Public Problems in a Shared-Power World.* San Francisco: Jossey-Bass, 2005.

Crouch, William H., Jr., and Joel C. Gregory. *What We Love About the Black Church: Can We Get a Witness.* Valley Forge: Judson, 2010.
Davis, D.B. *The Problem of Slavery in Western Culture.* Ithaca: Cornell University Press, 1966.
———. *Slavery and Human Progress.* New York: Oxford University Press, 1984.
Dawson, Michael. "A Black Counterpublic? Economic Earthquakes, Racial Agenda(s), and Black Politics." *Public Culture* 7.1 (1994) 195–223.
Dollard, John. *Caste and Class in a Southern Town.* New York: Doubleday, 1937.
Douglass, Frederick. *Life and Times of Frederick Douglass.* New York: Croswell-Collier, 1962.
DuBois, W.E.B. *The Negro.* New York: Oxford University Press, 1970.
———. *The Negro Church.* Atlanta: Atlanta University Press, 1903.
Dyson, Michael Eric. *I May Not Get There with You: The True Martin Luther King Jr.* New York: Free, 2000.
Eberly, Don E., ed. *The Essential Civil Society Reader: Classic Essays in the American Civil Society Debate.* New York: Rowan & Littlefield, 2000.
Fauset, A.H. *Black Gods of the Metropolis: Negro Religious Cults of the Urban North.* Philadelphia: University of Pennsylvania Press, 1944.
Field, Andy. *Discovering Statistics Using SPSS,* 2nd ed. Thousand Oaks, CA: Sage, 2005.
Fields, Bruce. *Introducing Black Theology.* Grand Rapids: Baker Academic, 2001.
Foner, Eric. *Reconstruction: America's Unfinished Revolution, 1863–1877.* New York: Harper & Row, 1988.
Franklin, Robert M. *Another Day's Journey: Black Churches Confronting the American Crisis.* Minneapolis: Fortress, 1997.
———. *Crisis in the Village: Restoring Hope in African American Communities.* Minneapolis: Fortress, 2007.
Frazier, E. Franklin. *The Negro Church in America.* New York: Schocken, 1963.
Frazier, E. Franklin and Lincoln, C. Eric. *The Negro Church in America/The Black Church since Frazier.* New York: Schocken, 1974.
Freedman, Samuel G. *Upon This Rock: The Miracles of a Black Church.* New York: HarperCollins, 1993.
Gadamer, Hans-George. *Truth and Method,* 2nd Revised Edition. Translated and revised by Joel Weinsheimer and Donald G. Marshall. New York: Continuum, 2004.
Genovese, Eugene D. *Roll, Jordan, Roll.* New York: Vintage, 1974.
Glazer, Nathan and Moynihan, Daniel Patrick. *Beyond the Melting Pot.* Cambridge: MIT Press and Harvard University Press, 1963.
Goldschmidt, Henry, and Elizabeth McAlister, eds. *Race, Nation, and Religion in the Americas.* New York: Oxford University Press, 2009.
Gollwitzer, Helmut. *The Christian Faith and the Marxist Criticism of Religion.* New York: Scribner's, 1970.
Groves, Charles P. *The Planting of Christianity in Africa.* London: Lutter-worth, 1958.
Guder, Darrell L. *Missional Church: A Vision for the Sending of the Church in North America.* Grand Rapids: Eerdmans, 1998.
Gutierrez, Gustavo. *A Theology of Liberation.* London: SCM, 1974.
Hamilton, Charles V. *The Black Preacher in America.* New York: William Morrow, 1972.
Harding, Vincent. *There Is a River: The Black Struggle for Freedom in America.* New York: Harcourt Brace, 1981.

BIBLIOGRAPHY

Harris, Fredrick C. *Something Within: Religion in African-American Political Activism.* New York: Oxford University Press, 1999.

Hauerwas, Stanley, and L. Gregory Jones, eds. *Why Narrative?* Grand Rapids: Eerdmans, 1989.

Heidegger, Martin. *Being and Time.* Translated by John Macquarrie and Edward Robinson. New York: Harper & Row, 1962.

Heifetz, Ronald A. *Leadership without Easy Answers.* Cambridge: Harvard University Press, 1994.

Heifetz, Ronald A., and Marty Linsky. *Leadership on the Line: Staying Alive through the Dangers of Leading.* Boston: Harvard Business School Press, 2002.

Hendricks, Obey M., Jr. *The Politics of Jesus: Rediscovering the True Revolutionary Nature of Jesus' Teachings and How They Have Been Corrupted.* New York: Doubleday, 2006.

Hessel, Dieter T., ed. *The Church's Public Role.* Grand Rapids: Eerdmans, 1993.

Hochschild, J.L. *Facing Up to the American Dream: Race, Class, and the Soul of the Nation.* Princeton: Princeton University Press, 1995.

Hodgkinson, Virginia A.. and Michael W. Foley, eds. *The Civil Society Reader.* Lebanon: University Press of New England, 2003.

Hooks, bell. *Yearning: Race, Gender, and Cultural Politics.* Boston: South End, 1990.

Hopkins, Dwight N. *Heart and Head: Black Theology Past, Present and Future.* New York: Palgrave, 2002.

———. *Introducing Black Theology of Liberation.* Maryknoll: Orbis, 1999.

Hopkins, Dwight, and George C.L. Cummings, eds. *Cut Loose Your Stammering Tongue: Black Theology in the Slave Narratives.* Maryknoll: Orbis, 1991.

Houghland, J.G., and J.A. Christenson. "Religion and Politics: The Relationship of Religious Participation to Political Efficacy and Involvement." *Sociology and Social Research* 67 (1983) 405–20.

Huggins, Nathan I., Martin Kilson, and Daniel M. Fox, eds. *Key Issues in the Afro-American Experience.* New York: Harcourt Brace Jovanovich, 1971.

Johnson, Charles S. *Shadow of the Plantation.* Chicago: University of Chicago Press, 1934.

Kaufmann, Yehezkel. *The Religion of Israel: From Its Beginnings to the Babylonian Exile.* Translated by Moshe Greenberg. New York: Schocken, 1972.

Kelsey, David H. *To Understand God Truly: What's Theological about a Theological School.* Louisville: Westminster John Knox, 1992.

King, Martin Luther, Jr. *Strength to Love.* Philadelphia: Fortress, 1963.

———. *Stride Toward Freedom the Montgomery Story.* New York: Harper & Row, 1958.

———. *Where Do Go from Here: Chaos or Community?* New York: Harper & Row, 1967.

Klarman, Michael J. *From Jim Crow to Civil Rights: The Supreme Court and the Struggle for Racial Equality.* New York: Oxford University Press, 2004.

Knoll, Mark A. *One Nation under God?: Christian Faith & Political Action in America.* San Francisco: Harper & Row, 1988.

Kotter, John P. *Leading Change.* Boston: Harvard Business School, 1996.

Küng, Hans. *The Church.* Translated by Rosaleen Ockenden and Ray Ockenden. New York: Sheed & Ward, 1967.

Lane, Robert E. *Political Life: Why and How People Get Involved in Politics.* Glencoe: Free, 1959.

LaRue, Cleophus J. *The Heart of Black Preaching.* Louisville: Westminster John Knox, 2000.

———. *Power in the Pulpit: How America's Most Effective Black Preachers Prepare Their Sermons*. Louisville: Westminster John Knox, 2002.

Lincoln, C. Eric. *Race, Religion, and the Continuing American Dilemma*. New York: Hill & Wang, 1984.

Lincoln, C. Eric, and Lawrence H Mamiya. *The Black Church in the African-American Experience*. Durham: Duke University Press, 1990.

Lindsey, William D. "Telling it Slant: American Catholic Public Theology and Prophetic Discourse." *Horizons* 22, 1 (1995) 88–103.

Linge, David E., ed. and trans. *Philosophical Hermeneutics*. Berkeley: University of California Press, 1976.

Lipset, Seymour Martin. *American Exceptionalism: A Double-Edged Sword*. New York: Doubleday, 1996.

Locke, Lawrence F., Stephen J. Silverman, and Waneen Wyrick Spirduso. *Reading and Understanding Research*. Thousand Oaks, CA: Sage, 2004.

Loewen, James W. *Lies My Teacher Told Me: Everything Your American History Textbook Got Wrong*. New York: Simon & Schuster, 1995.

López, Ian Haney. *White by Law: The Legal Construction of Race*. New York: New York University Press, 2006.

Lovin, Robin. "Civil Rights, Civil Society, and Christian Realism." *Religion and Values in Public Life (Center for the Study of Values in Public Life at Harvard Divinity School)* 6:2/3 (Winter/Spring 1998) 4–8.

Macaluso, Theodore F. and John Wanat. "Voting Turnout and Religiosity." *Polity* 12 (1979) 158–69.

Marable, Manning. *Living Black History: How Reimagining the African-American Past Can Remake America's Racial Future*. New York: Basic Civitas, 2006.

———. *Race Reform and Rebellion: The Second Reconstruction in Black America 1945–1990*. Jackson: University Press of Mississippi, 1991.

———. "Religion and Black Protest Thought in African American History." In *African American Religious Studies*, edited by Gayraud S. Wilmore, 318–39. Durham: Duke University Press, 1989.

Martinson, Oscar B., and E.A. Wilkening. "Religious Participation and Involvement in Local Politics throughout the Life Cycle." *Sociological Focus* 20 (1987) 309–18.

Marty, Martin E. "Religious Power in America: A Contemporary Map." *Criterion* 21, 1 (1982) 27–31.

Marx, Gary T. *Protest and Prejudice: A Study of Belief in the Black Community*. New York: Harper & Row, 1967.

Matthews, Donald R. and James W. Prothro. *Negroes and the New Southern Politics*. New York: Harcourt, Brace, and World, 1966.

Mays, Benjamin and Joseph Nicholson. *The Negro's Church*. New York: Russell and Russell, 1969.

McAdam, Doug. *Political Process and Development of Black Insurgency: 1930–1970*. Chicago: University of Chicago Press, 1982.

McCall, Emmanuel L. *The Black Christian Experience*. Nashville: Broadman, 1972.

Meachum, Jon. *American Gospel: God, the Founding Fathers, and the Making of a Nation*. New York: Random House, 2006.

Metz, Johann Baptist. *Theology of the World*. New York: Seabury, 1969.

Milbrath, Lester W., and M. L. Goel. *Political Participation*. Chicago: Rand McNally, 1977.

BIBLIOGRAPHY

Miles, M. B., and A. M. Huberman. *Qualitative Data Analysis: An Expanded Sourcebook* (2nd ed.). Thousand Oaks, CA: Sage, 1994.

Mitchell, Henry H. *Black Church Beginnings: The Long-Hidden Realities of the First Years.* Grand Rapids: Eerdmans, 2004.

———. *Black Preaching: Recovery of a Powerful Art.* Nashville: Abingdon, 1990.

Mitchem, Stephanie Y. *Name It and Claim It?: Prosperity Preaching in the Black Church.* Cleveland: Pilgrim, 2007.

Moberg, David O. *The Church as a Social Institution: The Sociology of American Religion.* Englewood Cliffs: Prentice-Hall, 1962.

Moltmann, Jürgen. *Theology of Hope.* New York: Harper & Row, 1967.

Morgan, Edmund. *American Slavery, American Freedom: The Ordeal of Colonial Virginia.* New York: Norton, 1975.

Morris, Aldon D. *The Origins of the Civil Rights Movement: Black Communities Organizing for Change.* New York: Free, 1984.

Morris, Aldon D., and Carol McClurg Mueller, eds. *Frontiers in Social Movement Theory.* New Haven: Yale University Press, 1992.

Myrdal, Gunnar. *An American Dilemma: The Negro Problem and Modern Democracy.* New York: Harper & Row, 1944.

Nelsen, Hart M., and Anne Kusener Nelsen. *Black Church in the Sixties.* Lexington: University Press of Kentucky, 1975.

Newbigin, Lesslie. *Foolishness to the Greeks: The Gospel and Western Culture.* Grand Rapids: Eerdmans, 1986.

———. *The Gospel in a Pluralistic Society.* Grand Rapids: Eerdmans, 1989.

Niebuhr, H. Richard. *The Social Sources of Denominationalism.* New York: Meridian, 1929.

Northouse, Peter G. *Leadership: Theory and Practice.* Thousand Oaks, CA: Sage, 2007.

Parks, Sharon Daloz. *Leadership Can Be Taught: A Bold Approach for a Complex World.* Boston: Harvard Business School Press, 2005.

Paris, Peter J. *Black Leaders in Conflict.* New York: Pilgrim, 1978.

———. *The Social Teaching of the Black Churches.* Philadelphia: Fortress, 1985.

Pascoe, Peggy. *What Comes Naturally: Miscegenation Law and the Making of Race in America.* New York: Oxford University Press, 2009.

Pattillo-McCoy, Mary. *Black Picket Fences: Privilege and Peril among the Black Middle Class.* Chicago: University of Chicago Press, 1999.

Patton, M.Q. *Qualitative Research and Evaluation Methods, 3rd Edition.* Thousand Oaks, CA: Sage, 2002.

Peterson, Steven A. "Church Participation and Political Participation." *American Politics Quarterly* 20 (1992) 123–39.

Pinn, Anthony B. *Terror and Triumph: The Nature of Black Religion.* Minneapolis: Augsburg, 2003.

Postal, Robert J., ed. *The Cambridge Companion to Gadamer.* Cambridge: Cambridge University Press, 2002.

Powdermaker, Hortense. *After Freedom: A Cultural History of the Deep South.* New York: Viking, 1939.

Proctor, Samuel D. *The Certain Sound of the Trumpet: Crafting a Sermon of Authority.* Valley Forge: Judson, 1994.

Putnam, Robert D. *American Grace: How Religion Divides and Unites Us.* New York: Simon & Schuster, 2010.

Rabinow, Paul, and William M. Sullivan, eds. *Interpretive Social Science: A Reader.* Berkeley: University of California Press, 1979.
Raboteau, Albert J. *Canaan Land: A Religious History of African Americans.* New York: Oxford University Press, 2001.
———. *Slave Religion: The "Invisible Institution" in the Antebellum South.* New York: Oxford University Press, 1978.
Rauschenbusch, Walter. *Christianity and the Social Crisis.* New York: Macmillan, 1907.
———. *A Theology for the Social Gospel.* New York: MacMillan, 1917.
Reed, Adolph, Jr. *The Jesse Jackson Phenomenon: The Crisis of Purpose in Afro-American Politics.* New Haven: Yale University Press, 1986.
Roberts, J. Deotis. *Black Religion, Black Theology: The Collected Essays of J. Deotis Roberts.* Edited by David Emmanuel Goatley. Harrisburg: Trinity International, 2003.
Roxburgh, Alan J., and Fred Romanuk. *The Missional Leader: Equipping Your Church to Reach a Changing World.* San Francisco: Jossey-Bass, 2006.
Savage, Barbara Dianne. *Your Spirits Walk Among Us: The Politics of Black Religion.* Cambridge: Belknap, 2008.
Schein, Edgar H. *Organizational Culture and Leadership.* San Francisco: Jossey-Bass, 2004.
Senior, Donald, and Carroll Stuhlmueller. *The Biblical Foundations for Mission.* Maryknoll: Orbis, 1983.
Sernett, Milton C. *African American Religious History: A Documentary Witness.* Durham: Duke University Press, 1999.
Simpson, Gary M. *Critical Social Theory: Prophetic Reason, Civil Society, and Christian Imagination.* Minneapolis: Fortress, 2002.
———. "God in Global Society: Vocational Imagination, Spiritual Presence, and Ecclesial Discernment." http://meh.religioused.org/GodGlobalCivil%20Society.pdf.
Sobel, Mechal. *Trabelin' On: The Slave Journey to an Afro-Baptist Faith.* Westport: Greenwood, 1979.
Smiley, Tavis. *How to Make Black America Better.* New York: Anchor, 2001.
Smith, Archie. *The Relational Self: Ethics and Therapy from a Black Church Perspective.* Nashville: Abingdon, 1982.
Smith, R. Drew, ed. *Long March Ahead: African American Churches and Public Policy in Post-Civil Rights America.* Durham: Duke University Press, 2004.
———. *New Day Begun: African American Churches and Civic Culture in Post-Civil Rights America.* Durham: Duke University Press, 2003.
Smith, Robert C., and Richard Seltzer. *Race, Class, and Culture: A Study in Afro-American Mass Opinion.* Albany: State University Press, 1992.
Stanton, Graham. *The Gospels and Jesus.* New York: Oxford University Press, 2002.
Strate, John M. "Life Span Civic Development and Voting Participation." *American Political Science Review* 83 (1989) 443–64.
Tanner, Kathryn. *Theories of Culture: A New Agenda for Theology Guides to Theological Inquiry.* Minneapolis: Fortress, 1997.
Tashakkori, Abbas, and Charles Teddlie. *Mixed Methodology: Combining Qualitative and Quantitative Approaches.* Thousand Oaks, CA: Sage, 1998.
Tate, Katherine, "Black Political Participation in the 1984 and 1988 Presidential Elections". *American Political Science Review* 85 (December 1991) 1159–76.
Thiemann, Ronald F. *Religion in Public Life: A Dilemma for Democracy.* Washington: Georgetown University Press, 1996.

Usry, Glenn and Craig S. Keener. *Black Man's Religion: Can Christianity Be Afrocentric?* Downers Grove: InterVarsity, 1996.

Van Gelder, Craig, ed. *The Essence of the Church: A Community Created by the Spirit.* Grand Rapids: Baker, 2000.

———. *The Ministry of the Missional Church: A Community Led by the Spirit.* Grand Rapids: Baker, 2007.

———. *The Missional Church & Denominations: Helping Congregations Develop a Missional Identity.* Grand Rapids: Eerdmans, 2008.

Verba, Sidney, et al. "Race, Ethnicity and Political Resources: Participation in the United States." *British Journal of Political Science* 23 (1993) 453–97.

Wainwright, Geoffrey. "Renewing Worship: The Recovery of Classical Patterns." *Theology Today* 48:1, (April 1991) 45–55.

Wald, Kenneth. *Religion and Politics in the United States.* New York: St. Martin's, 1987.

Washington, James Melvin. *A Testament of Hope: The Essential Writings and Speeches of Martin Luther King Jr.* New York: HarperSanFrancisco, 1986.

Welker, Michael. *God the Spirit.* Minneapolis: Fortress, 1994.

Welton, Donn. *The Other Husserl: The Horizons of Transcendental Phenomenology.* Bloomington: Indiana University Press, 2000.

West, Cornel. *The Cornel West Reader.* New York: Basic Civitas, 1999.

———. *Democracy Matters.* New York: Penguin, 2004.

———. *Prophesy Deliverance! An Afro-American Revolutionary Christianity.* Louisville: Westminster John Knox, 1982.

———. *Prophetic Fragments: Illuminations of the Crisis in American Religion and Culture.* Grand Rapids: Eerdmans, 1988.

———. *Race Matters.* Boston: Beacon, 1993.

Williams, Raymond. *The Long Revolution.* Westport: Greenwood, 1961.

Wilmore, Gayraud S. *African American Religious Studies: An Interdisciplinary Anthology.* Durham: Duke University Press, 1995.

———. *Black Religion and Black Radicalism: An Interpretation of the Religious History of African Americans.* Maryknoll: Orbis, 1998.

Wind, James P., and James W. Lewis, eds. *American Congregations Volume 2: New Perspectives in the Study of Congregations.* Chicago: University of Chicago Press, 1994.

Woodson, Carter G. "The Negro Church, an All-Comprehending Institution." *The Negro History Bulletin* 3, no. 1. (October 1939) 7.

———. *The History of the Negro Church.* Washington: Associated, 1921.

Yoder, John Howard. *The Christian Witness to the State.* Eugene: Wipf and Stock, 1975.

———. *The Politics of Jesus.* Grand Rapids: Eerdmans, 1972.

Zeuschner, Robert B. *Classical Ethics East and West: Ethics from a Comparative Perspective.* Madison: McGraw Hill, 2001.

www.ingramcontent.com/pod-product-compliance
Lightning Source LLC
Chambersburg PA
CBHW071453160426
43195CB00013B/2094